THE

FROM HEMORRHAGING

TO HEALING

Rhonda M. Joseph

Copyrights

For ordering, booking, permission, or questions, contact the author at **www.rhondajoseph.com**.

Unless otherwise indicated, Scripture quotations in this publication are from the King James Version.

ISBN # 978-1-7336635-0-2

Printed in the United States of America

DEDICATION

I dedicate this book to my precious mother, *Shirley Wilkins*, whose love and guidance have made me the person that I am today. From an early age, I watched you with admiration and respect, aspiring to someday be like you. You were my first teacher and have taught me so much about life, love, courage and the importance of working hard.

Through your struggles, I learned about perseverance and determination and how to never give up, even when others count you out. You have loved and lost but taught me to learn from every experience; not to forget but to forgive and "keep it moving." You've shown me what inner strength looks like. I love you more than words can say. *Through you I've learned that even when broken, not to stand still because it is possible to move from hemorrhaging to healing.*

ACKNOWLEDGEMENTS

This book has been like a fifteen-year pregnancy and while some would have wanted it to be aborted or miscarried, it has finally come time for delivery. As with any difficult pregnancy, it has come with highs and lows but the end result makes it all worth it.

Thank you, Cameron, Brandon and James, my heartbeats, my three sons, for loving me and allowing me to fulfill God's will for my life. You are my greatest gifts and it is a privilege and an honor to call each of you, Son. Always remember that with God ALL things are possible. Continue to allow God to order your steps. Keep stretching, keep reaching, you're almost there.

To my granddaughter, Jordyn, the sweetest girl I know, who came at a time when I needed to smile. The joy and love you bring to me is unmatched. I'll always be proud to be your "Gammaw."

To my three siblings: James Williams, Jr., Marion C. Jackson, Jr. and Tiffany Calloway. You are so precious to me. The love and laughter we've shared will always sustain me no matter where life takes us.

To my grandmother, Eliza Bradford, who gave me my greatest gift, an introduction to Christ. I'm forever indebted to you.

Your wisdom, prayers and love encourage me to love others unconditionally.

Most people only have one, but I've been blessed to have three dads pour into me, James Williams, Sr., Marion C. Jackson Sr. and Archie Wilkins. You have each played an instrumental part in me being who I am today and I'm grateful for your love and support.

God has blessed me abundantly with wonderful friends. I appreciate your encouragement and support. I am grateful for the sisterhood that I have with so many incredible women of God. I admire your gifts and cherish your friendship. To LaVada Johnson, Denise Wallace, Christina Davis and Angela Hasty, your friendship, encouragement and love have kept me moving when I wanted to stand still. Martina Young this book could not have been birthed without you and your wisdom. Thank you for being my first midwife. Tanya White thank you for the extra thrust I needed to push this out. Diane Beatty Corsey, thank you for always asking, "Is it finished?" "Are you done?" It motivated me to keep going.

Yvette Lewis, thank you for your assistance and patience in editing. I've learned so much about this process from your wisdom. Rev. Dr. Rick Hunter, thank you for being the theological professor that kept up with his student and encouraged excellence. Your wisdom and guidance were invaluable.

Words can't express the gratitude that I have for the wisdom that I have received from the most profound preacher of this century, my pastor, Rev. Dr. Kevin W. Cosby. I have benefited greatly from your teachings and under your leadership. It was under your direction that I realized it's not too late to go back to school or accomplish all the things God has for you.

To my father in the ministry, Wendell C. Lewis Sr., who has always encouraged me to preach and teach the uncompromised word of God. Thank you for believing in me from the beginning.

To my nieces and nephews, who allow me to be the "favorite aunt in the whole wide world." Your hunger and thirst for more help me to stay rooted and grounded wanting to be the example that you and others need. Thank you for loving me for me.

I take a minute to acknowledge those that walked away. Thank you for the life lessons. I'm better and stronger because of it. I'm not bitter but better. You prepared me for that one that was searching for his perfect match.

Finally, I give praise, honor and all glory to God for the Holy Spirit's guidance in writing this book.

FOREWORD

If given the opportunity to make the choice of being able to live our life without any troubles or anxieties, hurts or losses, or to live a life that has problems around every corner and breakdowns regularly, most rational people would choose a life without any problems or breakdowns. But do you personally know one grown person that has never had troubling challenges, hurts and betrayal, grief and despair?

Okay, you have the picture, life is a challenge to say the least and can be hell on earth at its worst. This book is about the reality of a life with challenges that could and would break the heart, mind and will of an individual…but it is also a book about what that life can become when Jesus is allowed to do triage on you right where you are in the battlefield called your life.

Triage happens when a war is going on. Medical doctors are stationed in makeshift triage tents as close to the battle as possible so that when a soldier is wounded she can get medical care as quickly as possible…the sooner the medical help, the better the chances are for a full and complete healing. In this book, Rhonda introduces you to one doctor, the only doctor of which it is said that he "can make the wounded whole."

A person once wrote:

"DO NOT JUDGE MY LIFE BY THE CHAPTER YOU WALKED IN ON."

Rhonda has given us compelling reasons why that statement is so true. Her personal journey from hemorrhaging to healing has all of the intrigue and despair of the "Housewives of Atlanta" meets Chris Rock's movie "I Think I Love My Wife." Rhonda takes the reader through a rollercoaster of highs and lows, laughs and tears, hurts and hate but she also brings you to the point where you can safely get off the rollercoaster ride and get on to an experience of healing, wholeness and thanksgiving…even if you are still without "him."

In Chapter One, you will be coached to acknowledge your hemorrhage and to own what you know about you. In Chapter Two, you will learn about the importance of getting a right diagnosis of your condition so that the prognosis will be the chance to experience a total recovery. In Chapters Three through Five you will learn about getting to the right doctor for your problems, how to live while you are in recovery and how hope works toward breakthroughs of healing.

In chapter Six, you will see with certainty that when Christ touches you, Christ enters into your pain…Christ takes on your pain, Christ gets in the yoke with you and brings you through the despair. In Chapters Seven through Nine, a picture is painted of how your hemorrhage can be transformed into a testimony of how the "truth shall set you free." Most important in this section is how the woman got her identity back…she was not any woman…she was God's daughter.

In the closing Three Chapters, Rhonda breaks

down the existential fear that your personal sin and doubt will keep you at a distance from God and that you will never be good enough to expect God to enter your personal hell and that is where you would be wrong. Rhonda shows you through what she has experienced, how she has hurt, what she has fallen for and that God has remained a confident conversation partner in her life journey. "She whom the Lord frees is free indeed."

This book shares with you the confidence of a weary prayer warrior, a discouraged mom, a frustrated single, that she knows how THIS Life story ends because she has already read the last chapter of God's book of grace…God and his children won.

If you need a spiritual B-12 shot to pick you up this book is just that.

Dr. Rick Hunter
Associate Professor of Theology
& New Testament Studies
and President, Sonforce Group
– *'engaging Christian leaders who are engaging
Christ with tools to engage the world'*

TABLE OF CONTENTS

INTRODUCTION

"Then the Lord God said, "It is not good that the man should be alone; I will make him a helper fit for him. So, the Lord God caused a deep sleep to fall upon the man, and while he slept took one of his ribs and closed up its place with flesh. And the rib that the Lord God had taken from the man he made into a woman and brought her to the man."
Genesis 2:18, 21-22

Let me tell you a story… a true story that helped me see me before it was too late for me to become her.

I recently read two of my journal entries that were dated August 20, 2011. The first one was written at 8:35 am. It started, "I'm sick of me. Eight and a half months later here I sat on my bed once again wondering how I got here. How do I keep holding out hope for a relationship that ended over a year ago? Lord, help me! It's hard to let go! I keep asking myself why it is so hard when you know you deserve to be treated better.

Why do you stay in that situation? Why do battered or abused women stay in marriages and relationships that cause them so much harm and pain – physically, mentally, emotionally and spiritually. Some for the

11

sake of their children, some for security, some for the sake of having someone. But is it more than that? Is it lack of self-esteem and when did it start?"

The second entry in the journal was written the same day at 8:08 p.m. and it discussed a 62-year old woman that God had allowed me to meet at church that evening, who needed a ride home. Through her, God would answer the very questions that I had asked that morning. She was in the entrance of the church asking anybody and everybody for a ride. I felt compelled. If you asked my sons, I was always compelled. The ride to her home while it was only about 10 minutes seemed like an eternity.

One minute I honestly believed she was mentally disturbed and the next minute highly intelligent. It was all kind of interesting. It was as if I was reading a book and I wanted to keep reading just to see what was going to happen next. I was intrigued. In that season in my life I was always wondering what God might be up to and what He might be doing, so I knew He had a purpose for me giving her a ride.

It's funny, like the woman with the issue of blood in the Bible, this woman will also remain unnamed. If we focus on her name or who she is, we might miss what God is saying to us through her story. We pulled up to her apartment and her dog was in the window, tangled in the blinds. I waited in the car while she rescued him.

She wanted to keep talking and something in me wanted to keep listening. She kept saying that she was hemorrhaging. She had used that word, hemorrhage the entire ride. I finally got enough nerve to ask her, "Why do you keep saying that you're hemorrhaging?" At that very moment, God gave me my purpose for her ride. She said, "I am hemorrhaging, and it still hurts so bad!" She proceeded to tell me that she had been in an abusive marriage for 40 years and had left. Her departure been two years prior, but it still hurt.

After 40 years of abuse, she got out. She ran. She couldn't take it anymore. She said her four children were grown. One was a doctor, one a lawyer but that all four were doing well. She confessed she should have left 20 years earlier when he broke her jaw, but she didn't because of the children and she had a good life.

I asked, "Good life?"

She said, "I had ten acres of land, nice home, nice clothes, etc."

I commented, "But no peace."

She said, "You're right." She invited me into what she called "her mansion." A small apartment but it was hers. It was full of papers, books, memorabilia, etc.

everywhere. Wall to wall papers. It all seemed chaotic. God let me know that even in what appears to be a chaotic and dysfunctional situation, if we're still, we can hear from him. I shared with her the title of this book and that it was about a woman who looked good on the outside but was bleeding and dying on the inside. She cried, and I cried.

I left her mansion and went home. I immediately looked up the definition of hemorrhage to get a full and clear meaning of the word. Webster defined it as a rapid and uncontrollable loss or outflow. I wrote in my journal, "My story is relevant. Yes, I am bleeding, and no one knows but so are a lot of women and they need to know that they aren't alone. Thank you, God, that you care about me – yes, disobedient, procrastinating, hard-headed me. Thank you for not giving up on me, even when I wanted to give up on myself. The pain has been great, the wounds are still open, the tears are still falling some days, but day by day I'm healing. Day by day I'm getting stronger. One day I pray the bleeding will stop."

Her story, my story, your story….

I've always desired to be married. To be a helper. To be connected to that special someone. I wanted to live happily ever after with my husband.

From the first time I heard that scripture in

Genesis 2, I knew I had been created for the purpose of being a wife and a helpmate. As far back as I can remember, I wanted that title and the responsibility that came along with it. I knew I was the rib that belonged to someone special; a God-fearing man that would love me as much as I loved him. I was determined to find that certain someone that I was specifically created for.

The search seems like it has gone on forever. One day, I was re-introduced to another scripture, Proverbs 18:22 that says, *"He who finds a wife finds a good thing and finds favor with the Lord."* What!!! *"He who finds…"* After all that time of looking, finding him wasn't even my job. That was the assignment of my husband-to-be, whoever he was and wherever he was. He would have to find me and know that I was his missing rib. It wasn't supposed to be me finding him and telling him that I was her. Was this really the way it was supposed to work?

I would have to wait for him to find me. Really? Because I didn't go many places, I didn't know how he was ever going to find me. We like to say we're waiting on God to send him, but we start trying to help by positioning ourselves in certain places, so we can be spotted. Some of us find ourselves in the club, posted up at the bar (and we don't drink), or at a sports bars (and don't even like sports), or at certain venues and dressed in the smallest or tightest clothing we can find trying to lure and entice that husband. We think he'll see me in here. I'll catch his eye. He wasn't necessarily looking for a wife, but you've now gotten his attention. He may not even be prepared for marriage, but you've decided he's the one and you can help get him ready.

As time passes, you wonder why it didn't work or is not working. Had you not captivated his attention by placing your protruding body parts in his face and space, you may not have endured some of the unnecessary stress and heartache he put you through. I believe a man will know when he is ready for marriage and won't have to be convinced that we are the one. When he is truly ready for a wife, he will go seeking for one. I do believe in positioning ourselves for the blessings of God. However, I also believe that we need to be led by God. *The steps of a [good and righteous] man are directed and established by the LORD, And He delights in his way [and blesses his path].* Psalm 37:23

After the man seeks and finds his wife, then the second portion of Proverbs 18:22 is realized – he has found a good thing (a rare treasure, a diamond, something of great value). He will realize that his newfound treasure is not something that he can easily walk past. He recognizes the true value of what is before him. You don't need to convince him that you're the one or that you're worthy and deserving of his love. He will have no doubt and will reassure you that he's the one that has been looking for you. Too often as women, we don't realize our value or worth and that's when and why we settle, compromise and start trying to make the connections ourselves.

Unless they are archaeologists, men aren't just looking for rocks; they're looking for that treasure. They are looking for their very own diamond. You may not be the biggest or brightest but the best fit for him. They are seeking to find that wife that will add value to who or what they are.

Once he has sought and found that good thing, then he will find favor with the Lord. Not only are you a good thing, but you are an added blessing to his life. He doesn't just get the gift of you - he also gains favor with the Lord. That's why a godly man isn't just looking for breasts and butt or someone who can just drop it like it's hot on the dance floor and that's the extent of their connection. He's looking for that good thing: the complete package, that wife that's multi-dimensional. She's not just good on her back but good on her feet as well. She may not be a gourmet chef, but can do a few things in the kitchen. She can hold a conversation about politics, sports, economics, etc. It may not be a lengthy conversation but she is not limited to talking about the latest reality show. She can work inside or outside the home. She is even good with math; she can add, subtract, multiply, and divide. She can add value by knowing how to bank, budget, balance and barter. She can reduce his worries and stress by knowing how to pray for his emotional and spiritual needs. She can multiply and increase his confidence by encouraging him to pursue his goals and dreams.

She reassures him that she'll be his biggest cheerleader. She knows their conversations are just that – their conversations, which are to remain private and not meant for public discussion at the beauty shop, over the phone with her girlfriends, etc. Finally, as a helpmate she can help him divide and conquer those things that would prevent him from reaching his intended destiny.

So now I must ask, "Do I really have what it takes to be a wife? Am I willing to cook a meal, or does he need to stop by the nearest drive-through? Am I willing to keep a clean house and launder his clothes (or at least get them to the cleaners)? Do I really want to be that Proverbs 31 woman? Do I really want to be a wife or just want that title?" Have I allowed him to find me or have I been doing all the seeking and finding? Have

I been trying too hard to connect to places where I didn't fit? Did I cause my own broken rib?

Instead of allowing the right man to find me, I was foolishly placing myself in a position to connect to men that were either not ready for what I was looking for and/or were never meant to be my husband. Little did I know, I wasn't as ready as I thought I was to wear or carry that title or position of wife. There was so much more development in me that was needed. I had to accept responsibility for my actions and not place the blame on anyone other than myself. I hadn't waited on God.

Don't get me wrong, I don't believe that men alone do the finding. I've come to learn that the teachings in Proverbs are truisms; meaning that they are normally true in the flow of life. So with that being said, "he who finds a wife finds a good thing" of course is not true of every man that finds a wife…although it is true for many. As a man moving in step with God is looking for a godly wife, the woman has a responsibility to be godly in her walk.

My personal issue is that I was doing all the seeking and finding and because I had not allowed God to do the leading, the end result was not good. I believed that I was meant to be a wife. I believed God had groomed me for Mr. Right but, unbeknownst to me, there was so much more grooming that needed to take place. Sadly, I didn't have the patience or sense to wait for God to bring us together.

I tried on numerous occasions to find him myself, but rather than finding Mr. Right, I found Mr. Right Now, Mr. Not So Right, Mr. He Just Won't Act Right, Mr. He Thought He Was Always Right, and lastly, Mr. I'll Be Right Back (not sure where he went because he never came back).

There were others - several others that weren't a great match. I tried way too often dating and connecting to men that were not meant for me. I continuously tried making the various relationships work. I tried making myself fit into his life/lifestyle only to find out I was trying to force something that was not meant to be. It's like trying to fit that square peg into the round hole.

No matter how hard you try or how many times you try - it just doesn't fit. After trying numerous times to fit where I didn't belong, I found myself weak, infirm and fractured. I had become "the broken rib."

My purpose for writing this book is two-fold: Obedience and Transparency. God's purpose for me writing this book is also two-fold: Deliverance and Healing. While I thought it was just about me, God is saying that it's bigger than me. The Lord told me to write this book over 15 years ago.

My first thought was, "Why me? Who would want to read anything that I've written?" I wrestled with not being good enough. Truth be told, writing this book was not the first time that I struggled with those thoughts of not being good enough. Writing would help me gain a confidence to say things that I'd held inside for many years.

God informed me that as I wrote, I would be healed and as you read there would be some things revealed to you about yourself that you might also receive healing and deliverance. Years later, He informed me that I wouldn't get married until the book was written. Out of delayed obedience, which I realize is plain disobedience, the book is now written. While I was given the title about 15 years ago, it took about 12 years for me to finally start writing this book. How ironic - 12 years!!!! It's ironic because the book would be based on a story from The Bible of the woman with the issue of blood, who had suffered for 12 long years.

After those journal entries, God spoke this is the intro to your book. The next day, He would give me some of the words for the back cover and table of contents. He let me know that I have either already lived or will live out each of the chapters between the intro and the back cover. That may have been part of the reason that I was slow to write. The journey had already been long and more than I had bargained for, I had no desire to endure more pain.

Today, I can say the pain has been great but not without purpose. The wounds have closed. Tears have been dried. The bleeding has stopped. I pray that as you read *The Broken Rib, From Hemorrhaging to Healing* (my story) that you may also receive any healing that you need from connecting to people, places and things that you were never meant to be entangled. The damage may not have been caused by connecting to the wrong man, but it could have been caused by attaching yourself to the wrong friends, job, church, habits, etc.

Let's take this journey together and move from hemorrhaging to healing. The journey for me has been a process and not an easy one. While this book won't take long to read, take your time. Read a chapter a day or week and meditate on each. At the end of each chapter, let's rate where we are in the process, using a scale from 1 to 10, we'll rate our level of pain. If you can be open and honest with yourself, I believe that you will receive healing that you may not even know was needed.

So, this is my story… a true story that helped me see (broken and hemorrhaging) me before it was too late for me to become (whole and healed) her.

*Heal me, O Lord, and I shall be healed; save me, and
I shall be saved: for thou art my praise.*
Jeremiah 17:14

Her story...............

Mark 5:25-34 King James Version (KJV)

[25] *And a certain woman, which had an issue of
blood twelve years,* [26] *And had suffered many things of
many physicians, and had spent all that she had, and
was nothing bettered, but rather grew worse,*
[27] *When she had heard of Jesus, came in the press
behind, and touched his garment.* [28] *For she said, If I
may touch but his clothes, I shall be whole.* [29] *And
straightway the fountain of her blood was dried up;
and she felt in her body that she was healed of that
plague.* [30] *And Jesus, immediately knowing in himself
that virtue had gone out of him, turned him about in
the press, and said, Who touched my clothes?* [31] *And his
disciples said unto him, Thou seest the multitude
thronging thee, and sayest thou, Who touched
me?* [32] *And he looked round about to see her that had
done this thing.* [33] *But the woman fearing and
trembling, knowing what was done in her, came and
fell down before him, and told him all the truth.* [34] *And
he said unto her, Daughter, thy faith hath made thee
whole; go in peace, and be whole of thy plague.*

CHAPTER 1: WHAT'S YOUR ISSUE?

*"And a certain woman, which **had an issue of blood** twelve years"* Verse 25

Have you ever had an issue that you thought would get better or go away within a day or two, but instead it lasted and lasted and lasted? You tried to fix it but no matter how hard you tried nothing changed. It caused you to lose sleep; caused you not to have an appetite and on some days, it caused you to overeat; caused you to have an attitude; it totally took you out of your element.

You tried to act like it wasn't affecting you but clearly you were not yourself. You couldn't talk to anyone about it because you knew they really couldn't relate or understand and even if they could, would it change anything?

In the fifth chapter of Mark, we find this unnamed woman who has been internally suffering for more than a decade. Her name isn't mentioned nor, does it give a description of her or any indication of who she is. Does it matter? Does she matter? No one knows the severity of her symptoms, the depth of her dilemma or the width of her wounds – only the length of her longsuffering. Some know that she has an issue but don't know the seriousness of her situation.

Because of this condition she has had to be isolated from family and friends. She can't go to work, to the store, to visit friends, etc. She has no one to talk to about what is going on with or inside of her. No one hears her cries for help. No one sees the tears that she's cried night after night for 12 long years. It is as if they are silent cries and endless invisible tears. She has an issue that is almost unbearable; an issue that has caused her to be lonely. This issue causes her to toss and turn and have restless nights. This issue has caused others to look down on her and place judgment. This issue has caused her to be broken; not just broken, but broken and bleeding.

The word *broken* is defined by Webster as *violently separated into parts, shattered, damaged or altered by breaking; having undergone or been subjected to fracture; violated by transgressions; discontinuous; interrupted; made weak or infirm; cut off; disconnected; not complete or full.*

The definition of *bleeding* as defined by Webster is *to emit or lose blood; to feel anguish, pain or sympathy.*

Have you ever gone through anything that left you

feeling broken: damaged, fractured, violated, weak or disconnected? Have you ever gone through something that caused bleeding: you felt anguish or pain? It's probably safe to say that if you've ever been broken, you also experienced the bleeding (anguish and pain).

We are told what her issue was - an issue of bleeding. The question is "What's your issue?" What has caused you to be broken? What has caused you to bleed? Are you broken and/or bleeding because of one of the following circumstances?

- Abandonment
- Abortion
- Abuse
- Addiction
- Being single – unattached
- Child out of wedlock
- Church hurts
- Death of a loved one
- Defamation of character
- Divorce
- Emotional instability
- Failed relationships
- Financial hardship
- Hurtful actions of someone you loved
- Illness (physical or mental)

- Incest
- Imprisonment of a loved one
- Inability to have children
- Infidelity
- Injury/accident
- Lies that were told on you/about you
- Loss of job
- Lust
- Miscarriage
- Molestation
- Rape
- Trauma
- Unplanned pregnancy

What has caused you to be weak or infirm? What has caused you anguish or pain? Was it one of these? A combination of these? Maybe, like me, it's been almost all of these.

Take a minute to identify YOUR issue. Not mine. Not your friends. Not your family members. Not that co-worker you could do without. Not even the church member that you wish had been there to hear that sermon pastor just preached. Not any of them. Put the focus on you. What's YOUR issue? Then answer the question, "How long have I been dealing with it?" It may have been just a week. One month. One year.

Maybe it's been 10 years or even longer. Can you pinpoint the issue and when it began? It's one thing to identify the issue, it's another to identify the inception – when and where did it all start?

My issue is that of being single. You might say, "Is that all?" But it's more than a relationship status. It's also the stigma that sometimes accompanies it. It's even more than that, it's dealing with why I feel like I shouldn't be single or can't enjoy life without being attached to someone. By no means am I saying it's my only issue, but singleness has been a major issue for me, more so than a lot of other things.

I felt like I needed to have a man in my life. I've settled, compromised, sacrificed and been hurt time and time again for the sake of being (or thinking I was) in a relationship. I've given my heart to men just to have it stepped on, crushed and returned to me on more than one occasion. It hurt and sometimes still hurts to think about some of my life experiences. It hurts when you give your all to someone – your time, your attention, your finances, your energy, your heart and your mind – all because you believe this is it. He's the one. This is Mr. Right. Just to find out that he lied to you, used you, mistreated you, abused you, cheated on you, etc. He's gone, and now you can't even think straight.

How could this happen……. again? I trusted him. He told me he had never met anyone like me. I had all the qualities he was looking for. No one went out of their way for him like I had. No one catered to him the way I did. Those are all the things he said. I didn't say it. He said it. I believed him. I trusted him. How could he do this to me? I put my dreams, plans, life on hold to help him with his. He could always count on me.

Hold on. It wasn't just one him. This isn't the first time. There have been several just like him. No one went out of their way for them like I had. No one catered to them the way I did. I trusted them. How could they do this to me? I put my dreams, plans, life on hold to help them with theirs. They could always count on me. Why couldn't it work both ways? We made plans. He was my future. One by one they were my future……. or so I thought.

Like this anonymous woman who had a constant flow of problems, I also have had a constant amount of issues that have kept me bound for longer than I probably care to admit.

Have you identified your issue?

Is it just one issue or are there multiple issues? How long have you been broken/bleeding? Do you remember the onset of this issue or condition? Did you really give it some thought? I did. Initially I thought I had been broken and bleeding for a short while, but I am now realizing that I've been bleeding for over 40 years. Yes, four decades.

I was four years of age when my daddy left me, not just me, but my mother and two-year-old brother as well. I remember it like it was yesterday. We came home and all of his belongings were gone and so was he. After frantically looking and searching the house, I also discovered that our piggybank (the Pringles can) was empty. The can was there but the money was gone. I waited for him to come back that night, even if he came without the money but he didn't. That's when the bleeding started.

I waited days, weeks, months, years, and decades for him to come back. My dad was a missing part of my childhood, my teenage years and part of my adulthood. How could he just leave without a word and not come back. No one knew how I felt. I don't know if I knew how I felt. I had never discussed it. My mother remarried, and I had a stepfather who provided for us, so I was supposed to be okay. Right? They provided all my needs and wants but there was still a void.

I always thought he would come back or show up at an event. I looked for him to show up at my fifth-grade graduation - he didn't. The bleeding continued.

I looked for him to show up at my eighth-grade graduation - he didn't. The bleeding continued. I never heard a word from or about him, but for some reason I had held on to hope. I just knew he would want to redeem himself and make every effort to be at my high school graduation - he wasn't. The bleeding continued.

At that point I hadn't seen or talked to him in over 13 years, but I just knew he loved me and would show up. After all I was his daughter. I was his firstborn. I was supposed to be daddy's girl, right? I was supposed to be the apple of his eye. But where was he? I was devastated. I was broken and bleeding. I was hurt. I was confused. I felt abandoned all over again each time something major happened and he wasn't there.

I screamed, "Help, can anybody hear me? I'm bleeding!" I'm crying. No one hears me. Are they deaf or are my screams silent? For years I had dreams of myself screaming to the top of my lungs and no one would ever come to my rescue. No one ever heard me scream. I'm realizing now, that in real life, I've been silently screaming and still no one hears me. No one comes to my rescue.

According to Jewish law, the woman with the issue of blood could not associate or socialize with others. This issue made her ritually unclean. She was an outcast. No one to hang out with. No one to talk to about what she was experiencing. No one to encourage her and let her know that they knew what she was going through. No one to give her hope in what appeared to be a hopeless situation. No one's shoulder to cry on. She's hurting. She's confused.

She's probably asking herself question after question, "Why?" "Why me?" "Why did this have to happen to me?" "What did I do to deserve this?" "How did I get here?" "How long will this pain last?" "When will it end?" "I've been there for everybody else, why isn't anybody coming to help me?" "How long must I go through this?" Have you ever found yourself in this place? Your mind is racing, blood rushing, you feel numb trying to figure it all out. You're alone. You have so many questions. You feel like an outcast. You still can't understand why or how you got here. You feel as though no one truly knows or cares about your issue or if they can really identify with who you are. You're not even sure who you are. Some people have judged you based on your issue or what they think they know about your issue.

She had 12 years of the same problem with no sign of things getting better. Day after day wanting someone to talk to, wanting someone to hold and embrace her, but night after night finding herself alone, feeling desolate, dejected and broken. Can you relate on any level?

No matter what it is or was that has broken you or caused you to bleed, look in the mirror, you're still here! God has a plan and purpose for your life. Jeremiah 29:11 NIV states, *"For I know the plans I have for you declares the Lord, plans to prosper you and not to harm you, plans to give you hope and a future."*

Despite everything you've been through…all the hurt, all the pain, every disappointment and every heartache, God still has a plan for your life. You could have given up. Some people thought you would or should give up. You may have wanted to throw in the towel. You weren't sure if life was worth living, but you hung in there, you stuck it out. You didn't quit, and God says, "I plan to give you hope and a future."

So, whether you've been broken or bleeding a month, two years, five years or like this woman, 12 years or longer, you've got to believe this too shall pass. You've been isolated and/or secluded way too long. You've been bound by this issue or sickness longer than you thought was possible. You want the bleeding to stop. You want the tears to cease and the pain to go away. You don't know when or how it will happen, only that it's necessary if you're going to live. You tell yourself, *"I shall live and not die,"* even though all the signs say the opposite.

It's the end of another day, somehow, some way you made it and then you are reminded of the scripture: *"Weeping may endure for a night, but joy comes in the morning."* Psalm 30:5

On a scale of 1 to 10, 10 being the worst, how would you rate your level of pain for the issue that you currently have or how would you have rated the issue that you had? _____

On a scale of 1 to 10, 10 being the worst, how would I rate my level of pain?　　　6 – 7

CHAPTER 2: GETTING WORSE INSTEAD OF BETTER

*"She had suffered a great deal under the care of many doctors and had spent all she had, yet **instead of getting better she grew worse.**"* Verse 26

Have you ever had a really bad day and thought to yourself (because you were afraid to say out loud), "What else can happen?" or "Can this day get any worse?" That's where we find this unidentified woman. Instead of things getting better, they were progressively getting worse. Not because of anything that she was necessarily doing but because of the actions of others.

Unlike some of us, she has come to grips with the fact that she has an issue. She is not in denial nor does she say, "It is what it is" and just accept that this is the way things are going to be. She no longer wants to have a pity party. She wants to get better. She has gone from doctor to doctor. She has gone to the local clinic, her primary care physician, all the referred specialists, trip after trip to the immediate care facilities and the emergency room. She has paid co-pay after co-pay and paid all the necessary out-of-pocket expenses. She has easily met her deductible year after year. She has filled every prescription that was written by physicians. She has tried every sample, over-the-counter, natural and prescribed medicine known to man and none of these have helped her issue.

Not only is she still sick in her body, but because of the numerous visits to these places, she is now sick in her finances as well. We've all heard the expression, "when it rains it pours." That was her current situation. She was having her own storm and didn't see an end in sight. It sometimes feels like trouble/pain is coming from every direction.

2 Corinthians 4:8 (NIV) says, *"We are hard pressed on every side, but not crushed; perplexed, but not in despair; persecuted but not abandoned; struck down but not destroyed."* Does it sometimes feel like the weight of the world is on your shoulders or that the load is just too heavy for you to carry? People try to encourage you with quotes and scriptures. *"Cast your cares on Him, his yoke is easy, and his burden is light."*

"He'll put no more on you than you can bear." You think they can't possibly understand what you're feeling or going through. This issue is not affecting just one area but several areas of your life. It's affecting you physically, emotionally, financially, socially and spiritually. No one realizes the agony that is taking place within. If they did, they would see that although you're still active in some areas, still going to work, still going to church, still taking your children to their activities, you're there physically but that's about all. Mentally and emotionally you're not even close.

This issue has had a domino effect. The woman with the issue of blood initially was just bleeding, but that one single issue has possibly caused other problems. Possible secondary issues: she's now anemic; withdrawn; financially bankrupt; emotionally drained; suffering from low self-esteem; battling identity issues and a victim of verbal abuse.

It's important that we identify the issue/problem but that's just the first step. If we want to get better, we must deal with the issue. Therefore, not only must we identify it, but secondly, we must attempt to look for ways to solve it. In school, the teacher would give a quiz or test that included word problems. I absolutely despised word problems. I would work the other part of the quiz or test first (true/false, multiple choice, fill in the blank) and always leave the word problems for last. They required too much time and too much thought. Occasionally, I would have time to work on them. Most often, I would not. I would sit at that desk, hoping by the time I got back around to those questions that one of three things had happened: the questions had changed, they were gone, or someone else was magically going to answer them for me.

I'm realizing that I've had that same mentality in life. Solve the easy stuff first and hope that the other stuff would just change, go away or someone else would come along and solve it for me. Not dealing with it doesn't make it go away. Not opening the bills, doesn't make them go away. Not taking the call from the collection agency, doesn't erase your debt. Not returning the doctors phone call, doesn't change your diagnosis. It only prolongs the inevitable and oftentimes makes things worse. Even dealing with it the wrong way can make it worse.

You may have only had one or two issues initially, but when left undealt with or mishandled, you now have another list. Not only do you have those original issues, but now you may be dealing with................

- Anger
- Anxiety
- Being Withdrawn (emotionally, physically or spiritually disconnected)
- Bitterness
- Communication (you're either too vocal or not vocal enough)

- Denial
- Dependency on people, places or things
- Depression
- Destructive behavior towards self or others
- Doubt
- Emotional Instability
- Exhaustion
- Fear
- Frustration
- Guilt
- Harmful habits
- Hate
- Humiliation
- Identity Issues
- Infidelity
- Insecurity
- Insomnia
- Lack of confidence
- Lack of or decrease in faith
- Loneliness
- Lying
- Paranoia
- Pride
- Promiscuity
- PTSD
- Regret
- Shame
- Trust Issues
- Unforgiveness

This list can be as long as the first one, if not longer all because we either ignored the primary issue or didn't properly handle it. Do any of these ring true for you?

How has your issue(s) changed you or your day to day life? Is life the same or has it grown worse? The changes could be subtle but you're not the same.

My issue of singleness and desiring to be married has cost me in many areas. It has had a domino effect. Sometimes we want what we want, and we'll do what it takes to make it happen. It may not necessarily be what's best for us but it's what we think we want and need at that moment.

Singleness led to loneliness. Others around me had their mates. I wanted mine. I desired to be married. I didn't want to be the only one without. I wanted to be married and thought it was the thing to do. I found myself engaged and with the help of my family (who had no idea I was broken and bleeding), I planned a wedding. Within six weeks I went from single to married. The domino had fallen. My desire caused me to marry prematurely. We were not equally yoked (not on the same page spiritually or emotionally) and, within a few years my marital status would change again…married to divorced.

During my marriage, I was involved in a serious

car accident. I broke 3-4 ribs, my pelvic bone, right wrist, punctured my bladder, not to mention the loss of pints and pints of blood. Now, not only was I bleeding emotionally, I was literally bleeding internally. The doctors said that the loss of blood had been substantial and I needed a blood transfusion. I begged them not to do it. They were insistent that it must be done.

I remember talking to my mom and stepdad and pleading with them to change the minds of the doctors. I recall asking them to give me until morning and if my numbers weren't elevated to where they needed to be at that time then they could proceed with the blood transfusion. They agreed. I remember laying in that hospital bed praying harder than I've ever prayed before all throughout the night. I remember saying, "I'm covered by the blood (the blood of Jesus). I quoted any song or phrase that I could think of about the blood of Jesus. "O The Blood," "Nothing, But the Blood," "There's Power in the Blood," "The Blood Will Never Lose Its Power," and "The Blood Still Works." The blood, the blood, the blood. The next morning when they checked my levels my numbers had doubled. THE BLOOD STILL WORKS!

I wasn't out of the woods as far as some of the other health concerns but I knew God was on my side and listening to my prayers. I didn't know how or when

I would be healed but I began to repeatedly say, "I don't know how but I know who." I knew who would heal me. I didn't know how long it would take but I knew who would do it.

I remember the excruciating pain of the broken ribs. I recall them working on all other parts of my injured body except for my ribs. No surgery. No wrapping. No taping. Nothing. I was told they would heal in time. Time? How much time? How long would my ribs be broken? How long would I remain broken? How long would I hurt? How long would I be in pain? How long would I suffer with a broken rib in the flesh as well as the spirit? I had a whole new set of questions and only God had the answers.

My issue of singleness and desiring to have a mate has cost me valuable time, energy and money. Furthermore, it has caused me heartache, stress, anxiety, high blood pressure, headaches, migraines, weight gain, weight loss, pain and suffering. This same issue caused me to use poor judgment, lower my standards, compromise, lose self-esteem, fornicate, commit adultery, lie, etc. It turned me into someone I didn't like or could barely recognize when I looked in the mirror. Those closest to me had no idea of the internal struggle I was battling. I may have looked good on the outside but there was a serious war going on in the inside that was slowly killing me.

Prolonged pain caused me to go into depression. I went from Singleness to Loneliness to Emptiness. I don't know how many of you know that you can get married and still experience singleness and loneliness, if he's not the one God intended for you.

Things had taken a turn ......they were getting worse instead of better.

Like this anonymous woman, I've been from place to place looking for relief. I've been to Bible Studies, Prayer Meetings, Tent Revivals, Retreats, Seminars, Church Conferences, Women's Conferences, Singles Conferences, State to State, Church to Church. Looking and searching. I would leave feeling (or appearing to feel) better for a while but still sick; still needing to be healed.

I wanted more! I needed more! I knew I desired more. I knew I deserved better than I had settled for. I also knew I was hurting. I was sick. I just wasn't sure how to get what I needed to receive my healing. I felt as though I was drowning, and I was going under further and further, deeper and deeper. I didn't have a life vest nor did I know how to swim. Once again, screaming but no one could hear me.

Thinking about where your issue started and how

it progressed:

On a scale of 1 to 10, 10 being the worst, how would you rate your level of pain? _____

On a scale of 1 to 10, 10 being the worst, how would I rate my level of pain? 10

I hurt all over – mind, body and soul.

CHAPTER 3: PRESS YOUR WAY THROUGH

*"When she had heard of Jesus, came in the **press** behind and touched his garment." Verse 27*

Have you ever got to the point where you were sick and tired of being sick and tired? You've had just about all you can take of a person or situation and you know it's time for something to change. You're not sure how but you know it's time. It's time out for thinking about it.

It's time out for talking about it. It's time to make it happen......and by any means necessary. Desperate situations call for desperate measures.

I remember getting to a place of being sick and tired of being sick and tired. I was dating a guy that didn't want to do much. He was content watching the 1970's sitcom, Good Times. I was tired of hearing about the characters and what they were doing. How many times can you watch the same rerun? I finally told him I was tired about hearing about good times and was ready to start having some good times. At some point, I needed to decide: am I sick of him or sick of me and my poor choices? My life was a rerun of choosing to date the wrong guys.

I've dated a truck driver that drove me crazy. Military men that either gave me an honorable or dishonorable discharge. A singer that dropped me like a mic and left me singing the blues. A sanitation worker that was full of garbage and dumped me. A guy that possibly spent a lot of time at the gastroenterologist because he was so full of crap. One that must have been studying to be a proctologist because every time you turned around he was looking at somebody's backside. A couple of them failed to mention that they doubled as magicians – they were good at disappearing acts. Don't let me mislead you, I'm not without fault and there were those times when I held the magic wand and caused some to disappear.

I certainly dated (not slept with but dated) a variety of guys. I had a type that I liked but I did not discriminate. I dated some tall, some short. Some light, some dark. I dated some that were in church as well as some that were not. I can't say that the ones that were not in church every Sunday were worse than the ones that were. That would be a false statement. Just because you meet him/her in church doesn't mean they were Heaven sent. Some people are in church preying and not praying. Some said that they were saved but couldn't really define what that meant.

By no means am I saying everyone I dated was a bad guy, they weren't. Most of them had really great qualities. I just wasn't the right fit for them. Had I not been trying so hard to connect with people and allowed myself time to properly heal after each relationship, I would have been more prayerful and discerning. I also realize that people can only do what you allow them to do. If you choose to be a door mat, know that you will be walked on.

When people show you who they are believe them. Quit making excuses for them. Quit lying to yourself. If you choose to be the weekend girl, the part-time lover or Tuesdays special, then that's all you will ever be. You have to know your value! For so long, I didn't know my worth.

In Genesis 2:22, God could have chosen any bone he wanted from the man to create woman. He didn't use the leg, arm, foot, etc. He purposefully chose the rib from his side. Textbooks indicate that the primary purpose of the ribs is to enclose and protect the chest cavity where the vital organs (heart and lungs) are located.

Thinking back to that time after the accident, it's hard to imagine that my ribs were serving their purpose of protecting and covering anything in their broken state. It was hard to get comfortable with ribs that were broken and not in their proper position. I constantly focused on the pain I felt and when I wasn't doing that, I was unknowingly causing pain to others. I would use pillows and blankets to try to prop myself up to find the most comfortable position. Most of the time it didn't feel natural; but felt awkward. Although I was not very comfortable I felt it was as good as it was going to get, so I settled right there.

I now know that I've literally been doing this same thing with men and dating. I've been this broken rib that was out of position. I've tried to forcibly make myself fit where I didn't belong. I told myself I was comfortable and while it didn't feel natural and sometimes even awkward, I believed that it was as good as it was going to get, so I settled right there.

Like my ribs, I've been broken and out of place for a long time. I don't believe I fully protected those things/people that were important and vital. How could I? I was damaged. While I prayed and tried to shelter and protect them, I pray that my sons weren't damaged because of some of my decisions. God once gave me a sermon entitled, "What will your disobedience cost me?" What will others suffer because I'm not in position? Stop and think about the affect your disobedience and being misaligned could cost someone else?

I occasionally wonder: *Have I left the heart of my future mate exposed and unprotected because I've been out of position? Has he received unnecessary heartache because I wasn't properly connected?* I can only pray that God has guarded and/or healed his heart. Being in position is essential.

As time passed I realized the doctors were right about my broken ribs. After months of being immobile, I did heal physically, but not without a lot of pain and suffering; not without self-medicating; not without doing a lot of crying when no one was looking; not without going through depression. I would lie on my side and press the broken ribs into the mattress to trying to position them in a way that I could get some relief. I tried to find some form of comfort. I was pressing into the pain. I was trying to press pass the pain. Stabilizing the broken ribs against the mattress was just a temporary fix but it brought relief. Have you ever self-medicated? How many times have temporary fixes brought you relief? No matter what the immediate remedy (drugs, alcohol, sex, etc.), it didn't last.

Can you imagine 12 years of mess? 12 years of

going through the same mess with no end in sight. They say that insanity is doing the same thing over and over expecting a different result. If that be the case, let me share a secret with you.......... I've been insane, certifiably crazy for a long time. I've subjected myself to so much unnecessary heartache and pain.

I remember one hot summer day that I decided that I had enough. It was time for me to get my life in order. I was no longer going to fulfill the lusts of the flesh. No longer was I going to be his Tuesday mid-day lunch special or his Friday late night snack. My days of being his Plan B were over. I had heard a preacher on a gospel television station say, "I will not compromise my long term goals for short term pleasures."

I remember writing it down, posting it on the mirror, memorizing and living by that phrase. If I wanted to be wife material, I needed to stop compromising with people who weren't ready to commit. That very day I decided to become celibate. I wasn't sure how long it would last but I had to try. One day went by; then a week; then a month; then two months; then a year and then two years; then another year and then another.

Four whole years I was on a roll until I wasn't. How do you get four years of being strong and determined under your belt, just to fall and find yourself right back at square one? I was mad at myself. It might not have been so bad if it hadn't been with the same person I had walked away from four years prior.

I was mad, angry, frustrated and hurt. Why do you keep making the same mistake? How do you keep going backwards? How do you keep getting stuck? I had been stuck but I knew it was time to move. I had set up residence in that place of pain far too long. Time to relocate. Time to strike while the iron was hot. No time to pack and bring anything extra. I needed to travel light. I beat myself up for a while. Then I realized if I was strong enough to last four years I could do it all over again, and so I started that journey again.

There are three things to consider in this chapter from that one verse (When she had heard of Jesus, came in the press behind and touched his garment). The first is that this anonymous woman had *heard of Jesus*. She had heard of His power. Maybe she heard how he had cast out demons or how he had healed the lepers or caused the blind to see, the deaf to hear, the lame to walk or how he spoke to the sea and calmed the storm. Whatever she had heard about him convinced her that it was time to relocate from her current situation and head into a new direction. She had a made-up mind. She decided that if things were ever going to change that the change must start with her.

She decided, "If I want something different, I've got to do something different." Possibly she recited the Serenity Prayer: Lord, help me to change the things I can, accept the things I can't and wisdom to know the difference."

Secondly, *she pressed behind.* She wasn't trying to be seen or noticed. She wasn't interested in making a scene or creating a disturbance. She didn't have to be nor did she desire to be the center of attention. She had no hidden agenda or ulterior motives. She stayed in her lane. She positioned herself for a blessing. It wasn't enough for her to just hear what He'd done for others. It was time for her to find out for herself. It was time for her to get her own testimony.

We say we want change. We say we want to be healed. We say we want to be delivered. We confess that we are ready to come out of our current state or situation, but are we willing to do what it takes to get out of it? Are we willing to step out and position ourselves in a place to be blessed?

You have a destination to get to. It may have been delayed but it hasn't been denied. You may have gotten detoured and distracted, but it's still your destination and God is still waiting for you to arrive at that place. We may have to come out of our comfort zone if we are to get to our destination and receive all that God has for us. Your healing and deliverance may only come when you move away from the familiar. Your freedom or healing may be contingent upon you changing something, whether it is your job, school, home, church, friends, relationships, etc.

Sometimes we get stuck in a place. It's all we know. It's all we've been accustomed to. This is the way I've always done it (even though it's not working this way and hasn't for a long time). Again, if you want something different, you've got to do something different. Come out of that familiar place. You cannot continue to allow the pain to paralyze you or the doubt to derail you. No matter how bad it hurts or how scared you may be, you must push pass the pain or move with the pain/hurt/sickness.

In the twelfth chapter of Genesis, God told Abraham to relocate. He had to pick up and move away from family and friends to an unknown place. Abraham, out of obedience, packed up and moved out. He didn't ask a bunch of questions. He didn't ask for anyone's advice. He heard the voice of God and he moved and was blessed because of it. God had promised him something and Abraham positioned himself to receive the promise.

Have you heard the voice of God? What has God promised you? Are you in position to receive it? It doesn't matter how long ago the promise was made. *He is not man that He should lie.* If he said it, it shall come to pass. Your blessing may be tied to your pressing. You may need to move from that place you are so familiar and comfortable with to your place of promise. Change your position! For some it may not be your position that needs changing, but your thought process.

If you change your mind you might just change your life. She pressed behind. She acted. What action do you need to take to properly align yourself for the blessing that awaits you?

Thirdly, *she touched his garment*. She moved in faith. She didn't ask someone else to do it. She didn't wait for permission. It's time for you to take control of your situation. You've given others too much control for too long.

It's time to put one foot in front of the other and step out. It's time to take a leap of faith. It's time to take matters into your own hands. She took her hand, stretched it forth and touched his garment. It's time for you to stretch. Stretch out your arms and surrender. Stretch (increase) your faith. Stretch (expand) your belief. Stretch (renew) your mind. What might you receive if you stretch? Your long-awaited spouse? Your promotion? Your degree? Your deliverance?

Your healing? Wholeness in your marriage? Restoration of a relationship? Peace of Mind? Joy?

Are you sick and tired of being sick and tired? Make up your mind today. Take the necessary action(s) to stretch forth. Don't be concerned with who's around, who's watching, what they're going to think or what they're going to say. It doesn't matter. What does matter is your healing, deliverance, wholeness, peace and joy. It's all available to you if you want it; if you're willing to take a step and press your way through.

Have you been able to press your way through? Why or why not? Are you ready to stretch?

On a scale of 1 to 10, 10 being the worst, how would you rate your level of pain? _____

On a scale of 1 to 10, 10 being the worst, how would I rate my level of pain?   9

> *It really hurts; the pain hasn't gone*
> *but my self-pity has ended.*

CHAPTER 4: KEEP HOPE ALIVE

For she said, *"If only I may touch his clothes, **I shall** be made whole."* Verse 28

The conversation was long overdue. She hadn't been able to bring herself to have it previously, but today would be the day. She had to do it. It was imperative. She couldn't let fear paralyze her any longer. She would finally muster up enough nerve to do it.

The conversation wasn't going to be with just anyone. It wouldn't be with her sister; not her mother; not a sibling; not a co-worker; not a church member; not her best friend; not even the guy she desperately wanted to share her thoughts and spend a lifetime with.

This conversation she declared would be private, "just between me, myself and I." It wouldn't be just any kind of talk; not the usual conversation ("I can't …," "They said…," or "What if….,"). It would be a life changing conversation. It would be a positive self-talk. Sometimes it's necessary to have "the talk" or to have a "come to Jesus meeting" as they use to say. She may have desired to have the conversation with someone other than herself but due to her issue, she didn't have that luxury which was probably for the best. There was no one there to give their opinion. There was no one there to be critical or negative about her thoughts. There was no one there to discourage or discredit her as they often did, whether intentional or not.

You don't always have to go looking for an answer elsewhere. You possibly do that too often, looking for someone else to solve your problem, offer a solution or give you validation. Not today! Everything you need, God has given you. I'm not saying that he won't allow you to ask others, but sometimes we become reliant on them instead of Him. Other times we fail to take the time to look within for the answers we need. If we did, we might find out that God has already told us what we need to do.

Today, have a positive self-talk (key words: POSITIVE and SELF). Not the normal negativity that occurs or the pity party that you've become accustomed to attending. The pity party is over! Blow out the candles, bust the balloons, and tell all the "little voices" good-bye. It's a new day! The conversation had to start in her mind with her thoughts.

"For as a man thinketh, so is he…" Proverbs 23:7

She gathered her thoughts and had the conversation. It wasn't rehearsed or practiced, just necessary. We all need to have that talk. It can start simple and then go deeper, it just needs to be meaningful and not spent beating yourself up. It really doesn't matter whether it begins with verses you remember from childhood stories like "I think I can, I think I can," or scripture that you learned long ago like, "I can do all things through Christ who strengthens me." The conversation must start somewhere.

I know there are times when I must encourage myself. No one else can do it because they don't know I'm hurting, broken and bleeding. Even if they do know (or suspect it) they don't know to what extent I'm suffering. Just a side note: people aren't mind readers. There are some people that have been placed around you to assist you through difficult times and would love to help you if they knew what you were struggling with or if they were asked.

However, there are going to be times when no one is around or available and you're going to have to encourage yourself. The word *encourage* means to inspire courage. Although she was scared she began to move in fear. Sometimes the first move you make must take place in your mind. After you get a made-up mind, then it can get in your heart and ultimately move to your feet. You're going to have to sing your own song; realizing that there won't be a choir, band or praise team around to get you going. There may not be a pastor or minister nearby.

There may not be a Bible or inspirational book close by. You're going to have to rely on the scripture that's in you. That's why it's so important to read and study the word of God for yourself. It's not enough to just go to church on Sunday and listen to the preacher and think that's all you need. You need more. Showing up on Sundays might have been a good place to start, but at some point, you're going to need more.

It's like going to the bank to make a withdrawal; if you haven't made any deposits, you're going to leave there empty handed. You may not remember the scriptures in their entirety. You may not be able to recall the book and verse, but whatever you remember, speak it into your situation. *"Greater is he that's within me than he that's in the world." "The Lord is my shepherd, I shall not want." "No weapon formed against me shall prosper." "If God be for me, he's more than the world against me."*

We've all heard the saying "Keep Hope Alive." What is this hope that's needed? Webster defines *hope* as "desire accompanied by expectation of or belief in fulfillment; to expect with confidence." It's not enough to wish, dream, cross your fingers, knock on wood or passively rely on luck. You must expect with confidence that things will change; that circumstances will turn around; that this too shall pass and that the best is yet to come.

After talking to herself, she decided to move in faith. This woman said to herself, *"if only I may touch His clothes, I shall be made whole."* This was a life changing statement for her…and maybe we can best understand her statement by looking at it in the four actions that she took to place her faith at the feet of Jesus Christ, the Son of God.

- *If only I* – no one else can do it for me
- *May touch His clothes* – make the right connection
- *I shall* – I expect
- *Be made whole* – to no longer be broken

This one sentence was loaded with self-talk and hope. In a sense she said, *"No one else can make the right connection, I expect to no longer be broken."* This statement (this positive self-talk) would redirect her life.

If only I – She understood that she alone had to do this. She couldn't rely or wait on anyone else. She had sat back and left her destiny up to others for the last time. The door of opportunity had presented itself and she was ready to walk through it. There are so many times we talk ourselves out of something.

This would be the day that she would need to be her own biggest cheerleader. It was personal. If it's going to happen, I must do it. I CAN do all things through Christ who strengthens me. I am the head and not the tail. I am above and not beneath. I am the lender and not the borrower. I am fearfully and wonderfully made. I am a daughter of the King. I can and I will get through this.

May touch His clothes – make the right connections. She wasn't trying to touch just anyone or have just anyone touch her. She had been there and done that and gotten worse. This time she was reaching for hope. This time she was aware that she didn't just want a touch that would be a temporary fix. She wanted to get to the one that would make a permanent and lasting change.

I shall – I expect. There was no room for doubt; no room or time to second guess herself. No time to get approval. No time to get another opinion or validation. I (me/myself) declare and decree that things are about to change for the better. *"Now faith is the substance of things hoped for and the evidence of things not seen."* Hebrews 11:1

Be made whole – no longer be broken. There had to be an admission or acknowledgement of brokenness and hurt. There's no room for denial if you really want to be healed and made whole.

I had read this scripture many times and I never had it "speak" to me as it did today. This woman spoke life to her situation. You and I must do the same.

Proverbs 18:21a KJV says, *"Death and life are in the power of the tongue."* How many times have you spoke death into or over your life? You've done so every time you've said…." I can't," "I'll never have," "I'll never be as good as …." "I don't know how." No more! Today, speak life! Today, be made whole. We often block our own blessings with the words we use. We need to start replacing the negativity with words that have power and life. Words that inspire and encourage.

If you don't have or can't find the right words to say, find them in the scriptures. If we're going to keep hope alive, we have to know where to find hope. Hope can be found in the Bible. As I previously stated, it's important to read and study the word of God for yourself. You don't have to be a pastor, preacher or teacher to read and the study the Bible. Break the scriptures down verse by verse and then begin to apply them to your life.

For example, Colossians 3: 1-2 *If then you were raised with Christ, seek those things which are above, where Christ is, sitting at the right hand of God.* [2] *Set your mind on things above, not on things on the earth.*

Ask yourself, "What is this scripture saying to ME?" Then actually give it some thought. We can't be intimidated by the word. It's important for us to break it down so we know how to apply it to our lives. Without getting too deep, let's take a minute to look at this verse.

Notice in verse 1, that Paul says to "seek those things which are above" and in verse 2, to "set your mind on things above." In verse 1, Paul is encouraging the believer to desire (a better word in this text for "seek") the things from above. Part of keeping hope alive is the desire from above.

Don't give up if the desire is not always really strong or always dominant, the verse says seek, which is in the present tense meaning we are always seeking, that is, desiring that which is from above. Make that desire a daily part of your prayer, a part of who you are and want to be. In verse 2, Paul says that we are to "set our mind on things above," he is speaking of a person's values. Value (the word for "set") what is of God and from God. This valuing is something that is learned and loved. A good way to learn this attitude of valuing is to hang close to those who are working to do it and love it.

Remember you are in a battle with Satan and he is

not trying to let you go, so desiring and valuing are a journey that gets better as you travel the path toward God.

How do I set my mind on things above and not on earthy things? Visualize it. Set (fix or steady) your mind. Picture moving an item from a low point to a higher place. An example would be moving a glass from the table to the shelf in the cabinet. Now move it from the bottom shelf to the top shelf. It went from a low point to a much higher place.

Now, picture moving your mindset the same way. Yes, picture it. Now, take it a little higher. If your thoughts of yourself are low – move them higher. If your dreams or plans are low – move them higher. Set (fix or steady) your mind/thoughts. Set it on what? The verse tells you on the things above. What are the things above? If we keep reading the verse goes on to tell you what those things are not (earthly things). So the things, earthly things, must be below (lower than or beneath) the things that you should be focused on. The earthly things are those things that will bring temporary pleasure and enjoyment.

The mind must be given to God. It is in our mind that our new nature and our old humanness are intermixed. We have to change the things that we are thinking about and/or dwelling on. In our mind is where we choose whether to express our new nature in holiness or allow our fleshly humanness to act up and act out.

When a believer's mind is transformed, his/her thinking ability, moral reasoning and spiritual understanding are able to properly assess everything (not that you will always make the right or best choice but the goal is to get there) and to choose that which is godly. You may be trying to do all the right things and get all that you can from God by praying, attending worship services and conferences, etc. only to find out that you are good for a short period of time…. then slowly but surely, the "old you" shows back up and you want to do what you (or the world) wants you to do. Stay focused! If you find it necessary, read another scripture to study and apply and then another and another until you begin to not just read but live the word!

There is so much more that can be said about these two verses but I just need you to know that if we're going to have hope and keep it alive, we have to set our minds on the things above. It all starts with a transformed mind that is set on the things above and not just on earthly things that will satisfy our flesh. (When you get some time read verses 1-17 of this chapter of Colossians. Paul writes clearly that there are some things (personality traits, mental views and self-imposed limitations) that we attach to our view of self that then serve to pull us into destructive habits.

Paul says we must put off these things. As those things are being put off, Paul then states there are some things that we need to put on…things that help us to stay together and to rise higher.

1Peter 1:13 – *Therefore, prepare your minds for action; be self-controlled; set your hope fully on the grace to be given when Jesus Christ is revealed.*

Philippians 4:8 (NIV) *Finally, brothers and sisters, whatever is true, whatever is noble, whatever is right, whatever is pure, whatever is lovely, whatever is admirable—if anything is excellent or praiseworthy—think about such things.*

Stopping the hemorrhaging is predicated on the journey of transformation, which starts in the mind. As you give yourself to God, you see more of God in you and less of the old nature. No more negative talk. No more placing/misplacing blame. No more excuses. No more reminiscing about those low things that don't matter. No more should of, could of or would of. No more crying.

Be determined to muster up enough strength to encourage yourself. I had to, and you must as well. Your life depends on it. There's victory on the other side. You must tell yourself I shall not die but live. I AM the head and not the tail. I AM blessed coming in and going out. By His stripes, I AM healed. Do you desire to be healed? If so, speak life!

John 5:6 (NIV) Jesus asked the lame man by the pool, *"Do you want to get well?"* He's asking you today, do you want to get well? Jesus told the man, "Get up! Pick up your mat and walk." At once the man was cured, he picked up his mat and walked. Jesus is telling you as he told that lame man (and me) - no more excuses, if you want to be healed, GET UP! Jesus knew how long he had been hurting. He knew the man was lying there and felt hopeless. He also knew the man's desire to be healed. The man had been at the right place. He had been in position and finally it would be the right time. Jesus knows that you've been hurting, and He knows how long it's been, whether 12 years like the woman with the issue of blood, 38 years like this lame man, He knows and He cares.

He's seen you lying there, desiring to be healed. You've been at the right place (church, on the altar, conference after conference) and now it's the right time. The wait is over! Do you want to get well? Get up. Pick up your mat and walk. Even if you haven't been at the right place, it's not too late to get there. Get up, pick up your mat and walk!

Some of us have lost hope. We've been in the same place with the same issue for so long we don't see a way out. We've buried hope. We've allowed hope to disappear. We've got to get hope back. You must see hope as a person, a companion, your best friend. If hope starts to leave, go get her. If hope disappears, look high and low, never giving up until you find her.

If hope has been buried, dig her up and dust her off. If hope has died, yell for help, get the medical paddles and bring her back to life. Whatever you must do, whether it's to talk to a friend, pastor, therapist; relocate; fast and pray....... keep hope alive!

Are you ready to have that positive self-talk? Are you ready to keep hope alive?

On a scale of 1 to 10, 10 being the worst, how would you rate your level of pain? _____

On a scale of 1 to 10, 10 being the worst, how would I rate my level of pain?   8

The pain still exists, but I'm more hopeful
than I've ever been that my healing is near.

CHAPTER 5: THE BLEEDING
HAS STOPPED

*"And straightway the fountain of her **blood was dried up**; and she felt in her body that she was healed of that plague." Verse 29*

Straightway – *Immediately; At once; Instantaneously; Straightaway*

Imagine hurting/bleeding every day of the year for 12 long years (144 months; 624 weeks; 4,383 days) and then suddenly, without notice or warning, it stops. A miracle? A dream come true? A prayer answered?

The fountain of her blood. It didn't say faucet or spigot, but fountain. This hadn't been a small issue. It had not been a drip or a leak, but a problem that ran deep, that flowed constantly, that appeared to have no end, but in an instant had dried up. The fountain (*the source from which something proceeds or is supplied*) was dried up. What is the source of your bleeding?

We've all had small problems that we've had to endure and overcome, but what about having an issue that has flowed constantly day in and day out, appearing to never end. It has drained you, almost left you hopeless and some days gotten the best of you. Then somehow, some way it finally stops.

She felt in her body that she was healed of that plague, that sickness, that issue that had kept her bound for years. She felt it. No one had to tell her. When you know that you know that you know. You don't need anyone else to co-sign or confirm what has happened. She knew things had changed. She knew life would never be the same. She knew the bleeding had stopped. She knew she had moved in faith. She knew she had taken a chance.

She had moved out of her comfort zone and had done something different. She had kept hope alive. She had had a positive self-talk but knew that wasn't enough. It was a good start but she had to do more than talk about it. She would have to move in faith and that's exactly what she did. James 2:26 tells us that *"faith without works is dead."* That means that it's not enough for me to have faith that my situation can or will change, but I must put actions with that faith and do something.

For example, if I want a career or better paying job, I must do something other than pray about it. I may have to update my resume', apply for the position, take additional classes or enhance my skills. If I want to own my own home, I may need to work on my credit, start saving, contact a realtor, etc. If I want to lose weight, I may have to change my eating habits and stop eating so much fast food or junk food. I might have to start exercising. If I want a husband, I should quit wasting time dating people that aren't interested in being married and start preparing myself so that I'm ready when the husband comes along.

When she moved, the miraculous took place. The bleeding stopped! The pain she had endured for years had come to an end. Life as she had once known it and grown accustomed had changed in an instant. We often want miracles to take place in our lives, but don't want to go through anything. We want the pain and suffering to stop, but don't want to do anything different.

Often because of fear, we're scared to do anything different. Oftentimes, if you want something different you must be willing to do something different. It's been said, you can't conquer what you don't confront. We can't live in denial nor can we be irresponsible about handling the issues in our lives. We must take a stand and deal with them head on.

We can't continue to roll over and play dead. Some of us are merely existing; just going through the motions. We appear to be walking zombies. We're getting up, going to work or school, coming home, eating, watching T.V., going to bed and doing the same thing day in and day out. It's time to move! Just like this woman with the issue of blood, it's time to move in faith, so that the bleeding can stop.

"The thief comes only to steal, and to kill, and to destroy. I am come that they may have life, and that they may have it abundantly." John 10:10 NASB

After years of thinking about my biological dad and the conversation that I might have with him if ever given the chance, I finally had the opportunity….40 years later! Yes, at the age of 45, I would finally have the long-awaited conversation. Somewhere around the age of 35, I found out that he lived right here in the city. He had never moved away. He had always been in the vicinity, just miles away from me.

We've met on many occasions to have lunch. We've spent time together. He's spent time with my children – taken them fishing, etc. It's been good seeing the person that he is today. We've had many conversations, but never that heart to heart that I had always dreamed of having with him. Not the one that I would blame him or accuse him for anything. Just a conversation to talk. Just to share who I was and find out he who really was.

Several times I called him to set up a meeting or

date to do just that but when he answered, anxiety and fear would always rise and I would change my mind and we would just have a casual conversation about anything other than what was deep within me.

God really began to deal with me as I wrote this book. I had no idea the wide array of emotions that were inside me or how deeply rooted my pain was when it came to the absence of my biological father. As I began to write, God began to minister to me about things that I was holding onto but was completely unaware. I never hated my dad. I've always loved him and wanted him to come back. I always missed him and held out hope that he would return, and I would be able to tell him those things, but I didn't…. until just a few days ago.

I called him, and he answered, but he was on the other side of town. So once again, I was going to let it go but something inside me wouldn't let me. I built up enough courage to tell him that I needed to talk to him and that it was not an emergency but that it was important. We agreed to meet the next day.

After hanging up, I cried and prayed. Prayed and cried. I cried some more and prayed some more. The next day, I would do more of the same. I was concerned about how to start the conversation or what to say during the conversation. Anxiety was beginning to set in, but I knew it had to be done. I called him. He didn't answer. I left a message and said to myself, "oh well, I tried." I knew he would call back and he did. We met for dinner and there was a lot of small talk.

Finally, I said to myself, "ok, this is it." I began to tell him about this book and how God was dealing with me about past hurts and issues and how they had affected me and the decisions that I've made throughout life. I began to cry as I told him I loved him and always had. I shared how him leaving and taking our money with him caused me to want to "buy" relationships.

I thought if I spent money on men I could keep them or if I gave them money or whatever else they needed, it would make them stay. It didn't work that way. They would get what they could get and still leave. I told him how I continued this cycle for many years. I wasn't blaming him, but finally understood why I was allowing certain behaviors in my life. I tried to buy the affection of men to fill a void that was created 40 years prior. It was if a hole had been dug in my soul and continued to get deeper with each passing year.

We talked for a while about the twists and turns that we had found ourselves in over the years. He was totally transparent and shared with me things about him that I never knew. Painful memories that he could have easily kept to himself but wanted to help me understand his upbringing. He hadn't had a father in his life and didn't know how to be a father. He didn't make excuses or try to displace blame. He took ownership for his actions. We hugged and left with a better understanding of who each of us are and how we got to this point. We couldn't change the past but could build on the foundation that was laid that day.

I thank God I moved in faith. Straightway, I knew the issues that had consumed me for years would no longer hinder me. That fountain was dried up. I felt in my body that something miraculous had taken place. I was healed of certain issues. The bleeding had stopped. I no longer needed someone to fill a void just for the sake of saying I have a man in my life.

Whatever issues have had you bound, stuck in a place and unable to move forward, we bind in the name of Jesus. Matthew 16:19 says *"I will give you the keys (authority) of the kingdom of heaven; and whatever we bind [forbid, declare to be improper and unlawful] on earth will have [already] been bound in heaven, and whatever you loose [permit, declare lawful] on earth will have [already] been loosed in Heaven."*

So, we take authority and bind the hands of the enemy and everything he has tried to bring against you and take from you. We bind every lie that he's told you and tried to make you believe. We bind anxiety, fear, doubt, frustration, insignificance and insecurity. You will no longer live in bondage and depression. We loose God's love, peace, joy, boldness and healing power. We believe that today the bleeding has stopped. You can no longer allow fear, insecurity, doubt, anxiety or anything else to consume you. Today, you can move from fear to faith.

Today you can move from insecurity to independence. You can move from doubt to determination. Determined that the bleeding and everything it represents has stopped. Those things that used to have you confused, afraid, depressed or insecure will no longer have a hold on you. They no longer have your blood pressure up and your spirit down. There's something happening on the inside of you. You're not sure what, but something is different. The bleeding has stopped.

If you still feel as if you are bleeding, ask yourself, "why?" Are there unresolved issues causing the blood to continue to flow? Is there a conversation that you need to have with someone? Ask God to reveal it to you and then ask for the strength and boldness to do something about it. What the enemy tried to use to harm you has backfired. This will be the very thing that will catapult you into your destiny. God can turn it around for your good. The enemy wants to keep you stuck. He wants you to feel defeated. He wants you to feel that you can't move from your current position, but he is a lie. He would desire that you be content and not get all that God has for you.

You intended to harm me, but God intended it for good to accomplish what is now being done, the saving of many lives. Genesis 50:20 NIV

No weapon formed against you will prosper; And every tongue that accuses you in judgment you will condemn. This is the heritage of the servants of the Lord, and their vindication is from Me," declares the Lord. Isaiah 54:17 NASB

Sometimes, the bleeding has stopped but the pain is still there. As was the case when I broke my ribs and had internal bleeding. The bleeding had stopped but I continued to hurt for months. Maybe the person is gone, but you're still hurting. Maybe the abuse has stopped, but you still feel the pain. Maybe your circumstances have changed, but you still can't shake what happened. It may be a process that will take some time to work through. Don't be discouraged. Don't lose hope.

Take one thing at a time; one step at a time; one day at a time. It may even be one hour or minute at a time. Rejoice every step of the way. Be excited that the process has started, and the bleeding has stopped. God will complete the process.

For I am confident of this very thing, that He who began a good work in you will perfect it until the day of Christ Jesus. Philippians 1:6 NASB

On a scale of 1 to 10, 10 being the worst, how would you rate your level of pain? _____

On a scale of 1 to 10, 10 being the worst, how would I rate my level of pain?   6

The pain comes and goes,
but the bleeding has stopped.

CHAPTER 6: A SECRET TOUCH

*"And Jesus, immediately knowing in himself that virtue had gone out of him, turned him about in the press, and said, **who touched my clothes**? And his disciples said unto him, Thou seest the multitude, thronging thee, and sayest thou, "Who touched me?"*
Verse 30-31

Have you ever been touched and unaware of who had done it? Today I discovered a scratch on my arm that appeared to be two inches long, red and irritated. I'm not sure what happened. Someone could have done it subtly and I was unaware or I could have unknowingly brushed up against something. I'm not sure who did it or when or how it got there.

If I had to guess, I would say I possibly did it based on the length of my un-manicured fingernails. However, that's just a guess. Let me say that while some of the wounds we receive are self-inflicted many are not. All I know is something or someone touched me, and I was unaware that they had left a mark/scar and it's not the first time something like this has happened.

Maybe you can relate to being touched and unaware of who did it because you were the victim of rape or maybe you've been violated by someone whose identity was unknown to you. Maybe you were the victim of someone who inflicted pain and caused harm and/or took something from you.

Maybe you can't relate to that but can relate to having been touched and couldn't (or can't) tell who did it. *A secret touch*. Someone's touch may have started subtle but then you were violated.

Someone has robbed you of your innocence; possibly deprived you of your youth; and/or tormented you through your teenage years. They took what did not belong to them and told you not to tell. *It's a secret.* Telling you if you told – something even worse than what has already happened to you would happen to you or those you loved. First, you think how could anything be worse than what I've just gone through? Then you think that you don't want this kind of hurt to happen to anyone else.

So, you keep your mouth closed. You keep the secret. Some people have experienced an inappropriate secret touch and thought it was acceptable. They didn't feel the guilt, shame and other negative emotions because they thought what had happened was normal. There are several reasons for this. Either the perpetrator told them it was normal; the feeling that they received from the touch didn't cause physical pain; the touch possibly felt pleasurable or made them feel a certain way (loved, accepted, needed, etc.). It may not have been until years later that they discover that it was not the norm and that they had been violated.

By the time it's realized, the person that was violated may now have questionable behaviors of their own that cause additional damage to themselves or others. Examples of these behaviors are that they may have prematurely gotten involved in sexual relationships; started seeking that type of attention from others; become promiscuous; or possibly found themselves violating others the same way they've been violated. Some people may do just the opposite and withdraw and become quiet, shy and keep to themselves. Either way, if untold, it remains a secret touch.

Along with the secret, you keep the guilt, the shame, the low self-esteem, the insecurities, the doubt that people would believe that you were innocent and that you had done nothing to deserve what had happened to you. You keep it all. You hold on to it for years out of fear; out of frustration; out of wanting to avoid judgment. It would remain a secret touch.

Although you knew you should tell someone, you no longer knew who you could trust. You no longer knew who would keep you safe because the person that secretly touched you was your older brother, father, stepfather, uncle, cousin, family friend or ministry leader. For some it could even have been someone of the same sex. For some girl, it could have been an older sister, aunt, female cousin, your very own mother or grandmother. For some boy, it could have been an older sibling, uncle, male cousin, father, stepfather or grandfather.

It sounds unheard of, but it unfortunately is not uncommon. How could they have done this? How could they have violated me? How could they say they love me or care about me and do this to me and then swear me to silence?

Then more questions come to mind – how can I just keep silent? What did I do to deserve this? What role did I play? Is this my fault? Who should I tell? Everybody? Anybody? But because of fear…. nobody! It will remain – a secret touch.

You go on with life as if this part is separate from anything and everything else. Separate from school. Separate from work. Separate from all activities. Whether it happened once, occasionally, often or for years, it can't be your primary focus because it's a secret that you can't dwell on or share. So, you just go throughout life as though it didn't take place. You go to school. You develop friendships/relationships. You go off to work. You work and build a life and name for yourself. You exist with your secret.

Maybe you've never experienced that type of secret touch. Maybe just the opposite, you've longed for a touch. Maybe you've been at a point in your life where you needed a touch – not wanted but needed! Perhaps, you were married and or in a relationship and secretly desired the touch of your spouse/mate. You longed to connect with them physically and emotionally, but something was missing. You craved their affection and attention, but constantly left their presence feeling starved; lacking the substance that you thought you needed to be sustained.

For whatever reason, they couldn't or wouldn't fill that void. You've possibly expressed your feelings and concerns, but they've gone unheard or at least have not been reciprocated. What used to be a thriving, fulfilling relationship now has you longing for a touch. You're almost ready to settle or compromise for any old touch, but you know that any touch won't do. Any touch won't satisfy. You need a touch that's powerful. You need a touch that's purposeful and you know you can't just get it from anybody. Truth is you don't just want it from anybody.

In attempts to find healing, this woman with the

issue had been touched by several people. Now it was her turn to do the touching. Without anyone knowing, this woman who had suffered for 12 years with the same issue, conjured up enough strength to push pass the crowd, stretched forth her hand and as the King James Version says, "touched the hem of his garment." A secret touch. It appeared no one knew who did it. To touch the hem of his garment, one would assume she was in a low position on her knees or even prostrate.

That should be a reminder to us that sometimes it's necessary to get on our knees or lay prostrate before God to get what we so desperately need. We may need to humble ourselves before the Lord to make our requests known to him.

"Seek ye first the kingdom of God and his righteousness and then all these things shall be added unto you." Matthew 6:33

Pride can cost us our blessing, our healing, our breakthrough. We can't be so high and mighty that we fail to bow down to the one who is still restoring sight to the blind, causing the lame to walk and raising people from their death beds.

This anonymous woman wasn't loud. She wasn't trying to be seen. She wasn't seeking attention. She just believed if she could get in the presence of Jesus and just touch his garment, her life would be changed.

Without warning or notice – there was a secret touch. The verse said that "Jesus, immediately knowing in himself that virtue had gone out." No one told him he had been touched. He knew within himself.

When you know that you know that you know, it doesn't matter what anyone else says or thinks. There was no doubt in his mind that he had been touched. Jesus knew he had secretly been touched and that there was an exchange that had taken place. Jesus had lost virtue. She had found healing. What she had been longing for years was finally taking place. She would no longer have to subject herself to unkind words or unhelpful people. She had received the very thing she had longed for – healing! Not from a man or medical doctor but from the Great Physician himself.

Jesus asked, *"Who touched my clothes?"* Thinking it odd, giving the surroundings and masses of people, the disciples said, *"you see the people crowding against you and yet you ask, who touched me."* (NIV) They couldn't understand how Jesus could ask such a question. To them the question was absurd, but to Jesus it was a valid and completely legitimate question to ask. He knew he had been touched.

Sometimes, even those closest to you don't know you've been touched. They've been around you for years and think they know everything there is to know about you. They believe they know you better than anyone else. These same people vow to have your back. They say they'll always be there. They say they'll watch and pray. Those friends and family members that you've been around for years have no idea of all the things you've truly endured. Not one of them knows that something has happened that has changed your life or your perspective. Not one of them saw it happen. It really was a secret touch.

There wasn't just a touch. The same moment that she realized that the blood had dried up Jesus also knew something had just transpired. There had been an exchange.

Have you ever purchased something from a store and had to return it because for whatever reason it didn't meet your needs? You return to the store where you originally bought the item just to find out that they don't give refunds but will allow an exchange. It may not be what you had in mind, but you agree to the exchange. You search until you find something of equal value. You leave satisfied. You feel as though it was an even exchange.

A different scenario would be that you purchased an item and have to return it. When you get to the store to do so, you see they are having a huge sale. Not only do you get your money back for the item you previously purchased, you also leave with a couple of extra items that you weren't expecting to buy. You leave feeling good about what just happened. That's what happened with this woman with the issue of blood. Not only did the bleeding stop, she received something extra.

The touch may have been a secret to others, but Jesus is aware of what has taken place. He knows about your secret touch. He is aware of the touch that occurred back then and is equally aware of the touch that you need today.

Was there a secret touch? Is it still a secret?

On a scale of 1 to 10, 10 being the worst, how would you rate your level of pain? _____

On a scale of 1 to 10, 10 being the worst, how would I rate my level of pain?   5

The bleeding has stopped, and He knows
I've made the right connection.

CHAPTER 7: YOU CAN'T HIDE FOREVER

*"And he looked round bout to see her that had done this thing. But the woman fearing and trembling knowing what was done in her, **came and fell down before him**." Verse 32-33a*

In the previous verse, Jesus asked, "Who touched my clothes?" But here we read, "He looked round bout to see *HER*." Jesus undoubtedly was aware of who had touched His clothing. He knew a woman had pressed through the crowd and had touched him.

Others had looked over her. They had looked past her. They had looked around her. They had looked down on her. Jesus intentionally looked to see her that had done this thing. He looked not with discontent or disgust but with compassion. He sought her out. He purposed to lay eyes on her.

With fear and trembling, she came out of hiding. She could no longer allow fear to be a factor. She could not be concerned about what the people were thinking or what they would say or do. She came fearing and trembling. She moved with fear. She moved in fear. She moved!

You can't let anything, or anybody keep you

stuck. As hurt as she had been and as much pain and heartache as she had endured over the years, she conjured up enough strength to move past all of that and move towards her healing. Not only did she have strength to press past the hurt, lies, deceit, etc., she had found courage from deep within to make her way to Jesus. She tapped in to her inner strength. She realized that *"greater is He that's within me than He's that's in this world.* (1John 4:4)" She was stronger than she thought she was or stronger than people gave her credit for and so are you.

We can't let the opinions of others keep us from receiving what God has for us. Too many times we are more concerned about what they will say than we are about getting the healing or deliverance that we need. We think they may talk about us or tell someone else about us. We're concerned about being embarrassed or ridiculed. The truth of the matter is that they are probably already talking about you, but you can't let that stop you from getting what you need. I see so many people come in church hurt, broken, depressed and the unfortunate thing is that they leave out the same way that they came in. They're too afraid to ask for help or prayer for fear someone may see them in a negative light if they knew what was going on with them. So, they wear a mask in and wear that same mask out.

The verse says knowing what was done "*in*" her, she came and fell before him. During her lifetime, she had endured many things. There was so much that had been done to her that affected the way she had lived. Something changed on the inside of her that would change how she would think; how she would live; how she would communicate with others from that day forward. She would no longer be the victim. She would no longer be a second-class citizen. She would no longer be defined by her condition. She would no longer focus on the things that had been done to her, but her focus would switch to the things being done within her.

She had finally come out of hiding. Some of us have been hiding in the shadows or in the background for a long time. Some of us at home. Some of us at work. Some of us in the church. Wherever the location, we've been hiding out. Not wanting anyone to know who we really are. Not wanting to reveal where we've been or what we've gone through.

I couldn't hide forever. You can't hide forever. You can't conceal the molestation, rape, adultery, bouts of homosexuality, promiscuity, repossessions, imprisonments, addictions, abuse, etc., forever. You can't continue to hide behind the guilt, shame and/or embarrassment. God is trying to move you from that place. He's moving you out of your comfort zone. He's pulling you out of those familiar places and away from those familiar people, places and things. He's trying to move you from defeat to destiny. From pain to purpose. You can't remain stagnant. You can't remain in bondage.

It's time to break loose from those things and people that have shackled you, causing you to be immobile and remain where you are. Some of us have become accustomed to taking a backseat behind others. God has called you into leadership, but you are afraid what people will say or what they will think. Therefore, you just sit on your gift. You fill other roles on the job or in church, but not what He purposed for you to do. You do a great job, receive accolades etc., but there is a void because that which you were created to do has not been fulfilled. You long for more. You need and desire more but are afraid to step out and get it. Jesus is calling you, *"Come out, come out, wherever you are – you can't hide forever!"*

She would take another step of faith. The first one was when she pressed her way past the crowd to Jesus. This time she would take a step and move in fear and fall at his feet. In humility, she bowed down before him. She was not concerned about being exposed, ridiculed or scorned. She stepped out of her safe place. She came out of hiding.

At some point, you must move into or at least move towards your destiny. There's no more hiding in the shadows of others to make them look or feel good. No more hiding behind pride. No more hiding behind fear. No more hiding behind shame, embarrassment, doubt or anything else. You've been in hiding long enough. She fell at His feet. I'm sure she had fallen at the feet of others before, possibly begging and pleading for help, just to come up short; just to remain in the same hopeless situation.

She humbled herself. She bowed down before the Lord. It was as if she were saying, "I've tried to do this on my own and come up short time and time again. I surrender my life to you. No longer will I hide behind people or issues. Heal me. Cleanse me. Forgive me. Whatever you need to do, do it! I just want to be free."

On a scale of 1 to 10, 10 being the worst, how would you rate your level of pain? ＿＿＿＿

On a scale of 1 to 10, 10 being the worst, how would I rate my level of pain? 4

I'm no longer bleeding or hiding, but I'm scared of what happens next.

CHAPTER 8: NO MORE SECRETS

*"**And told Him all** the truth." Verse 33b*

All – *the whole amount, quantity or extent of*
Truth –*that which is true or in accordance with fact or reality*

She told him all – the whole amount – everything - the good, the bad and the ugly. Not just the part she thought he would like to hear. Not just the part that would make her look good or portray her as a victim. Not just the part that that those who were listening would give approval of or smile about. Not a half or partial truth. She told him the whole truth.

It was confession time. She told him about all of her issues, past and present.

- It was me that had been abandoned
- It was me that had the abortion
- It was me that they abused
- It was me that was verbally abusive
- It was me that struggled with addiction
- It was me that caused him to become addicted
- It was me that wrestled with being single
- It was me that was the victim of church hurts
- It was me that caused some church hurts
- It was me that stole it

- It was me that started the rumor or kept the

gossip going
- It was me that experienced defamation of character
- It was me that cheated and caused the separation/divorce
- It was me that was on a roller coaster because of emotional instability
- It was me that tried to hang on to failed relationships when you said no
- It was me that was/is drowning because of financial hardship
- It was me that endured the hurtful actions of someone I trusted
- It was me that longed for that imprisoned loved one
- It was me that had a hardened heart after the loss of a loved one
- It was me that cried because of my inability to have children
- It was me that hasn't fully recovered from that miscarriage
- It was me that had a child out of wedlock
- It was me that caused his/her injury/accident
- It was me that told lies
- It was me that was negligent
- It was me that was filled with lust or fulfilled someone else's lustful desires
- It was me that secretly slept with their spouse
- It was me that refused to apologize
- It was me that chose not to forgive
- It was me that was molested or inappropriately touched by someone else

- It was me that was raped or violated
- It was me that touched him/her inappropriately
- It was me that suffered with sickness/disease
- It was me that went through depression
- It was me that contemplated suicide

At that moment it all came out. She had so much to say. Words that she had never shared with anyone else were finally articulated. She was finally in the presence of someone who really wanted to know what was going on with her.

Things that had been bottled up for years came flowing out. She told him all the truth. She told him who did it. She told him when it all started. She told him what happened. She told him where it happened. She told him how it all transpired. She told him where all she had gone trying to get help. She explained that she had went to family and friends. She acknowledged that she had sought professional help. She confessed that she had even looked for unconventional aid, but nothing had worked. In fact, her situation had not gotten better, but with time had only gotten worse. She explained despite her situation, she continued to try to live as normal of a life as possible, but realized she wasn't living at all, but was merely existing and found herself not even doing that well.

She let him know that over the years, she had experienced so many emotional highs and lows. The lows far outweighed the highs. It was as if she had been fastened to the biggest roller coaster ride known to man. She had been up, and she had been down. She had experienced disappointment, heartache, sorrow, anger, bitterness, loneliness, depression, doubt, shame, fear, distrust, frustration, embarrassment, regret, low self-esteem and the list went on. No matter what remedy she tried the roller coaster ride seemed to be without end.

Have you ever felt like this woman? You might have gone to family members, friends, co-workers, church leaders, doctors, even talked to complete strangers about your situation and things didn't change. You may have tried to get relief through alcohol, drugs, sex, pornography or even shopping. Like her, your situation only got worse instead of better. These may have been temporary fixes that brought minimal relief, if any at all. You were merely putting bandages on situations that required surgery. You were tapping into what you thought were reasonable resources. You may have gone to different places and tried various alternatives, not realizing you were causing more suffering. She needed to get to the source, which was Jesus.

When she opened her mouth to speak to Him, she didn't realize she had so much to say. She didn't realize she had been holding in so much for so long. Sometimes, we hold things in or keep them to ourselves for so long that we don't realize the internal damage that has taken place. We develop headaches, depression, anxiety, gastrointestinal problems, etc. Sometimes, we may not realize that we are still holding on to some things. What things have happened in your life that you are still holding on to and haven't dealt with or resolved?

What if you opened your mouth and begin to tell all the truth? Were you molested? Inappropriately fondled? Raped? Abandoned? Mistreated by siblings/parents? Bullied in school? Ridiculed? Did you try drugs and become addicted? Did you abort or miscarry a child? Were you given away as a child? Have you endured the loss of a child/parent/ or other loved one? Were you physically abused? Mentally or verbally abused? Maybe you've mistreated someone through words or actions and haven't dealt with it. Whatever it is, you can tell God ALL the truth. After all, He was there. He saw it all. He knows it all. He may want you to verbalize it to Him in order to receive your healing.

Psalm 34:8 *The LORD is close to the brokenhearted and saves those who are crushed in spirit.*

1John 1:9 says, *"If we confess our sins, he is faithful and just to forgive our sins, and to cleanse us from all unrighteousness.*

Notice I said He may want you to verbalize it to

Him. This verse says that she told Him all the truth. Sometimes telling the wrong person or people can make your situation worse. Take Joseph for instance. In Genesis 37, he shared his dreams with his brothers. After hearing what Joseph said, his brothers conspired to kill him. After discussing it, they decided not to kill him but to throw him in a pit. They didn't stop there but went further and sold him into slavery.

Not everyone can handle your story, your vision, your dream or your secret. Be careful who you share it with. It's not to say that God doesn't want you to share it with anyone. He may need you to use wisdom and discernment as to who that someone might be.

Earlier in chapter 2, we read that this woman had suffered under the care of many doctors and instead of getting better, she grew worse. She had told her problems to people with positions and titles. People she thought would have a solution to her problem but did not. We often do the same, just to be let down. Matthew 6:33 says "seek ye first, the kingdom of God and His righteousness; and all these things shall be added to you."

Seek Ye first. Not your best friend, boyfriend, spouse, parent, colleague or pastor. Ye being God. She had been suffering 12 long years. I just wonder if instead of seeking the help of people if she had sought the help of God first, would she have suffered as long? Just a thought. Whose help are you seeking or have you sought? I know you've possibly gone to others, but have you gone to God with all the truth? With all your problems? With all your fear?

Sometimes, God will do the healing himself. Other times, He may have us to go to someone else such as a doctor, counselor, pastor, teacher, etc. I believe if we seek him first, He will guide us to the right doctor, counselor, pastor, teacher, etc. Who has God released you to share your hurt/story/vision with and how much, if any have you shared? Something happened when she told ALL the truth. Something happened when she was no longer concerned with hiding her feelings but became transparent about what was happening inside of her. Something happened when her healing was more important to her than her pride. Something happened when she was no longer worried about what people would say or think. Something happened when there were No More Secrets! She felt lighter. When she released some things, it would then make room for the things that God wanted to release to her.

The second part of verse 33 of Matthew says, *ALL these things will be added.* What things? Healing! Deliverance! Prosperity! Peace! Joy!

Restoration! Love! Marriage! Degree! What things are you waiting for? We want Him to add the things without us first seeking Him but that's not the way it works.

1Peter 5:7 says *"Casting all your cares [all your anxieties, all your worries, and all your concerns, once and for all] on Him, for /he cares about you [with deepest affection, and watches over you very carefully].*

Again, the word is specific – ALL and HIM! Tell Him your secrets. Tell Him all – the whole truth. Truth – *sincerity in action.* She didn't give him part of the story, but humbled herself, risking shame and condemnation. She had taken the advice of others and had tried to fake it until she could make it, but she was tired and wanted to be free. She wanted to take off the mask. She was exhausted putting on a façade. She was ready to come clean with the only one to whom it really mattered.

She told how she desired to be in a long-lasting relationship but had found herself in countless meaningless associations with people who had used her. She told him how she had given more to others than she should have. She had been lonely. She just wanted to be loved. She just wanted what she saw others with. She longed to have someone she could call her own.

She told how she had cried herself to sleep

countless nights waiting for someone to call. She had friends that were happily married or engaged to be married and she was happy and excited for them but wondered if she would ever get a turn. She told him about the bad relationships she had been in prior to knowing her worth. She told him of the loneliness and anxiety she experienced while waiting to be healed. She told him how she was hurting and that she was yearning to be loved.

Longing for something that would last longer than just a season. It was no longer a want but something she needed. She needed Him to know that she was hurting and no longer concerned about what others would think if she told her whole story. Not just the parts she had told her girlfriends about but the whole truth.

What secrets are you holding on to? What skeletons are lingering in your personal or family closet? How long have you been holding on to this secret? Who or what are you protecting by keeping this secret? Are these secrets keeping you in bondage? Are you ready to be free? Let this be the day that you tell HIM all the truth.

It was going to be easy for me to end this chapter right here not dealing with my secret. The secret that I kept for many years. I can understand why people keep secrets, especially if it will affect or hurt those that you love. I had held on to this for so long and not shared it with anyone; but even I didn't know I was keeping a secret. Let me explain.

The memory had been suppressed for so long that I didn't recall it until a turn of family events caused it to surface. The thought of a young family member being touched or violated the way I had as a child brought memories back that I had long forgot. Along with the memory came fear, anxiety and questions. What would people say or think? How could I have forgotten something like that? Even as I type, those same feelings and questions rush in consuming my thoughts and wanting to overtake me. Although, I had to tell a few people in order to avoid history repeating itself, it wasn't made known to everyone in the family. It was on a need-to-know basis. Only those directly affected would need to know. I felt like it protected the perpetrator. I've never been one for confrontation. I wasn't mad at him. How could I be? I had not remembered and over the years I had been interacting with him as if nothing was wrong. I had bottled-up the events and the threats of harm that had come along with them. Who would believe that it really happened? Who would believe that someone they all knew and loved would do such a thing? Not just a friend of the family but an actual family member. I believe that the women of the family chose to handle it. I think they confronted him. After all, it was the women who handled most things in our family.

I was living out of town when the memory resurfaced. I recall talking to one of my aunts on the phone and felt paralyzed when she told me that he was going to watch her children while she worked. I became speechless. I remember hanging up but becoming fearful. I wanted to do something but didn't want to do anything at the same time. I prayed about it for some days. Sometimes that's all we think we must do but sometimes God requires that we do more than pray. I remember calling a different aunt who was also living out of town to share with her. She told me I had to tell the secret and if I didn't that she would. Within days it was out. *No more secrets!*

I remember them being concerned, confused and angry which were all valid emotions, but God was dealing with me in a different manner. I couldn't understand why they could be so full of anger towards my offender, but I didn't have the same response when my memory was restored. God had done so much for me over the years and he reminded me that His grace had been sufficient. He had been healing and protecting my mind even when I didn't know or remember. While I had made some poor choices as a teen and adult possibly as a result of being exposed to certain behaviors at the age of 7 or 8, God had been a keeper of my mind and heart. While my memory had been temporarily erased His love and forgiveness for my shortfalls had permanently been etched in my mind and soul.

But he said to me, *My grace is sufficient for you, for my power is made perfect in weakness." Therefore, I will boast all the more gladly about my weaknesses, so that Christ's power may rest on me.* 2 Corinthians 12:9

Thou wilt keep him in perfect peace, whose mind is stayed on thee: because he trusteth in thee. Isaiah 26:3

He that dwelleth in the secret place of the most High shall abide under the shadow of the Almighty. [2] I will say of the LORD, He is my refuge and my fortress: my God; in him will I trust. Psalm 91:1-2

While because of fear and uncertainty, I didn't necessarily want to come forward with what had happened back then and even now, God needed me to know that it would be my voice that would help or save someone else.

For God has not given us a spirit of fear, but of power and of love and of a sound mind. 2Timothy 1:7

For those who may not have had a voice or felt like they could speak, I did not have the luxury to keep silent. It was time for me to use my voice. For so long the enemy has wanted me to believe that I did not have a voice and for just as long, I have believed that same lie. God is reminding me that I do have a voice and that it should be used not to tear down or gossip. I have a voice that should be used to encourage, console, defend, speak truth, correct, rebuke, exalt, pray, teach, preach and prophesy at the very least. We must get to a place where we trust God with everything even when the people around us or closest to us may not understand; even when we can't share everything with everybody or anybody, we can pour out our hearts to God.

A time to keep silence, and a time to speak. Ecclesiastes 3:7b

Once she told him everything, he assured her that he was not like the others and that men were limited in what they could do, but his actions had shown her that with him, anything was possible.

"And Jesus looking upon them saith, with men it is impossible, but not with God: for with God all things are possible." **Mark 10:27**

On a scale of 1 to 10, 10 being the worst, how would you rate your level of pain? _____

On a scale of 1 to 10, 10 being the worst, how would I rate my level of pain? 3

I'm no longer bleeding, nor am I hiding or keeping secrets. I'm free but I'm feeling exposed.

CHAPTER 9: TRUE IDENTITY REVEALED

*And he said unto her, **Daughter...**" Verse 34a*

There were thousands upon thousands of people around Him, yet He directed His attention solely to her. He possibly had been touched by her story, maybe the fact that she was courageous enough to tell it in front of everyone. Maybe He was moved by the fact that she put her fear aside and pressed pass the crowds to get to Him. Maybe it was because she was bold enough to touch Him knowing that she was unclean. Whatever the reason, she had his undivided attention.

*He said unto her...*He didn't talk about her. He didn't speak to others regarding her. He didn't speak at her. He spoke to her. He directed his thoughts toward her and her alone. She was his primary focus. Nothing else mattered at that moment. It was personal. He called her Daughter. *"Daughter!"* Before He used this term, there had been no other word used to give reference to her identity. *Daughter!* Had she found the Father that she had longed for? *Daughter!* Did she now have a true connection with someone? *Daughter!* Did she now have a relationship? *Daughter!* Did she now have a sense of belonging?

How long had she wanted to be in a relationship with someone who truly cared, whether it was parental or relational (with a man or a good friend)? How long had she waited to hear someone claim her or reference her as family? How long had she wrestled with her identity? Who am I? So often we either forget or lose who we are.

Too often when circumstances change our identity changes. What happens when the titles, labels and positions that define us are stripped away? Pregnant for months and then there's a miscarriage – stripped of the title of mother. Happily married and then suddenly divorced – you are stripped of the title of wife/husband. You whistle while you work until you receive the pink slip – they take away your title of employee. You're excited about going to school until your financial aid runs out – now you're stripped of being a student. One by one our titles disappear and sometimes self-esteem and confidence leave with it and are replaced with fear and shame. You wrestle with your identity.

How did I go from student to drop-out or

employee of the month to unemployed? Our identity will constantly change if we are defined by positions and titles only. Life may throw us some curveballs and deliver the unexpected but we can't let that stop or define us. I am who God says I am. It's not what they call you but what you answer to. I am a daughter of the King.

Daughter! He called her Daughter. They had a relationship. A connection. That one word gave purpose. Gave hope. Gave direction. Gave destiny. It wasn't important what anyone else had called her before that moment. What she had been labeled prior to then was irrelevant and would no longer carry any weight. Once called "Unclean", but now called *"Daughter."* Once unknown or nameless, now recognized.

For years she was disconnected from society and from all social events, now she had a personal connection. She belonged.

For so long, she was known by her condition and circumstance. She had worn the title, Unclean, that they had given her and made her wear like a badge of dishonor for the last 12 years. She had heard them talk about her and her situation. She had heard the labels that they had placed upon her. She had listened to them for so long that she believed them.

She had accepted those names as her own. She knew that wasn't the name that she had started this life's journey with, but over time she stopped defending herself. She stopped trying to explain to people what had happened. She became tired. She became full of self-doubt. She became full of insecurity. She became full of shame. She began to walk with her head held down. She began to have low self-esteem. She had lost her identity.

From there, she would begin to wear a mask and try to hide or disguise the hurt and pain that she endured. No one would know how she really felt. If anyone would ask, "How are you?" She would respond, "Good," or "Okay" or her favorite religious response, "Blessed and highly favored." She got accustomed to her mask and hiding behind it.

From time to time, people would enter her life that she thought she could be totally transparent with and share how she really felt. Unfortunately, they had no regard for her issues and she would feel exposed and hurt time and time again.

These hurts would cause her to become more introverted and shop for a new mask. She vowed not to let anyone get close again. Not close enough to see her bleeding. Not close enough to see her hurting. Everyone she let in, let her down. She began to build a wall that would grow rapidly. With each hurt, the wall grew higher. With each rejection, the wall became thicker. To protect herself, she would keep people at arm's length. She had gotten good at wearing her mask. She did not let people know who she really was or what she had gone through.

The mask wasn't always comfortable. The mask wasn't always convenient nor was it attractive. But what the mask was, was safe! They couldn't see the scars behind the mask. They couldn't see the look of defeat. They couldn't see the doubt and fear and sometimes shame that consumed her. They couldn't see the tears behind the mask. The mask had become a permanent part of her wardrobe.

Today, someone saw pass the mask. It may not have only been what he said, but how he said it. It was loving and not loathing. He didn't say it with contempt but with compassion. It had been so long since anyone had acknowledged her less known speak with compassion.

He said, "Daughter." It was someone saying, "I accept you as you are. I'm calling you as one of my own. I'm here for you. As lonely as you may feel, you are not alone. We're in this together. We're connected. I know the struggle has been real. I've seen where you've been. I've seen what has happened to you. I've seen the tears. I've seen how they treated you. I heard how they talked to you."

But today God is saying, "I need you to listen to my voice. I'm calling you my own. I call you Daughter. I'm calling you into your destiny. I'm reminding you that you have purpose. Everything you went through was for a reason. It was not in vain. It was strengthening you. It was preparing you. It was helping you realize who you could and could not trust. It let you know who was really in your corner – who would be there with you or who would walk away when things got tough. Your hurts and responses to it helped shape your character. Your ability to overcome has developed your strength."

Romans 8:28 *"And we know that all things work together for good…"* All things. Everything you've been through. All things. Every hurt, every pain. All things. Everything you've overcome. All things. Every heartbreak. Every heartache. Every trial. Every tribulation. Every valley. Every dark place. It all will work together for good.

Not that all things would be good. Not that all things would feel good. But all things would work for good. No longer do you have to be confused about your identity. No longer do you have to be defined by what happened to you. No longer do you have to wear or hide behind a mask.

Today, you're called Daughter. It doesn't matter about the names or status of your biological parents. It doesn't matter if you were raised by foster or adoptive parents or a single parent. None of that matters. Today, you are called DAUGHTER, by the King of Kings, which makes you a princess. You are royalty!

You are royalty, not because of who you are or anything that you've done, but because of who God is. He wants you to know that you are valuable and that you are valued. Your past doesn't determine your worth. What happened to you in the past doesn't dictate what he has waiting in store for you.

The Lord says, "Forget what happened before, and do not think about the past. Look at the new thing I am going to do. It is already happening. Don't you see it? Isaiah 43:18-19a NCV

Your truest identity has been revealed. You are a Daughter of the King. Don't let anyone keep you in a place of not knowing your true identity. *"My people are destroyed for lack of knowledge."* You are who God says you are. Remove the labels that people have put on you. Remove the labels that you've even put on yourself. For so long, I didn't know who I was or if I had value. Was I important? Did I matter? Today, I know who and whose I am.

On a scale of 1 to 10, 10 being the worst, how would you rate your level of pain? _____

On a scale of 1 to 10, 10 being the worst, how would I rate my level of pain?   2

I'm no longer bleeding. No longer hiding.
No more secrets. I have an identity.

The question now ……. where do I go from here?

CHAPTER 10: FAITH HAS HEALED YOU

"……. thy faith has made thee whole" Verse 34a

Her faith had made her whole. Her healing had not come through doctors, medicine, magic or anything else. It was HER faith. Not her grandmother's faith. Not the faith of her parents, siblings, friends or her pastor. It was HER faith that had caused her to be healed. It was HER faith that caused her to be made whole.

The Bible gives scripture after scripture about faith. For those of you who don't read the Bible, this next scripture may be a new revelation for you. For those of you haven't read it in a while, this may be a refresher. For those of you who read the Bible, this may be a reminder for you.

So, whether it be a revelation, refresher or reminder, here it goes…. Hebrews 11:6 says, *"But without faith it is impossible to please him."* Him being God. It goes on to say that *"for he that cometh to God must believe that He is, and that he is a rewarder of them that diligently seek Him."* This one verse has 3 parts that we should consider:

A. Without faith it is impossible to please God.

What is faith? Merriam Webster defines it as something that is believed especially with strong conviction. Hebrews 11:1 says, *"Now faith is the substance of things hoped for, the evidence of things not seen."*

Faith is seeing it before you see it (you must see it in the spirit before you see it in the natural). Faith is believing in God and His Word. If He said it, it shall come to pass. It will happen. Faith is being confident that if He has been there for you in the past, that He will continue to be there in the present and the future. You must take Him at His word.

You must believe in His promises. So often we believe the promises of men before we believe the promises of God.

People have made us promises and have broken them time and time again. *God is not a man, that he should lie* (Numbers 23:19).

We must have faith to believe in His promises. It's our faith that pleases God. So many times, we try to please other people. I have spent a lot of years being a people pleaser. Maybe you can relate.

I would do what others wanted to do. I would go where others wanted to go. I would eat where others wanted to eat. I would put their wants, needs and desires before my own. I wanted to ensure their happiness. I wanted them to be happy or pleased with me. I'm not saying there is anything wrong with helping or making other people happy, but not at the cost of losing yourself. I began to make their likes my likes. Their dislikes my dislikes; failing to realize that what I liked and disliked also mattered.

At some point, I didn't know what I liked to do because I had always done the things that others liked or enjoyed. This wasn't limited to relationships with men but with most people in general. They could always count on me to be there to do the things that needed to be done or do the things that no one else wanted to do. I was a loyal and dedicated people pleaser.

I remember the day that I was liberated – set free. No longer the "yes man (or woman)." I said, "No!" I said the word and meant it. I'm not sure who was more shocked me or the person that the words were directed towards in that unique moment. From that day forward, I realized that I didn't have to always say, "yes" to what someone else wanted me to do. Saying no didn't make me a bad person (like my mind and others had deceived me into thinking for so long). I had always felt that I had to say yes –

maybe for acceptance or to be liked. Maybe to feel wanted or needed. I now know that the issue was more deeply rooted and went back to my childhood and not wanting to be rejected by anyone for any reason. Sadly, not wanting to be or feel rejected caused me to want to please others by any means necessary.

One day I came to the realization or should I say that God gave me the revelation that no matter how hard I tried to please people they may not be satisfied. When I stopped trying to please them and began to ask God to show me what pleased Him, my life changed. I was no longer in bondage to others and their expectations.

I'm not saying that I don't find myself regressing from time to time by trying to accommodate others. However, what I am saying is that as soon as I realize that it's happening, I try to evaluate the situation.

Am I (or my actions) saying yes because I genuinely want to do whatever is being asked of me or am I saying yes because I feel that's what the other person wants or expects? The inability or unwillingness to say no can cause more harm than good. I need to be more concerned with what God wants or says than people. We all do. Pleasing Him should be our top priority.

B. *He that comes to God must believe that He is.* He that comes to God. You must go to God. He is your source. How do you come to God? The same way she did. Humbly. In all honesty. In faith. With expectation (belief).

The way to go to God is through prayer. No matter what situation you face, you can talk to God about it by praying. You have to pray in faith, not just believing that he hears but that he will also answer.

You must believe that He is. He is what? He is able! Able to meet your needs. Able to make the crooked places in your life straight. Able to make the rough places smooth. Able to turn your night into day.

Able to make a way out of no way. Able to open doors that no man can close. Able to close doors that no man can open. We must believe that He is. He is a bridge over troubled water. He is a lawyer in the courtroom. He is a doctor when you're sick. *He is an ever-present help in trouble* (Psalm 46:1). He is Alpha and Omega. He is Jehovah Jireh – The Lord Provides. He is Jehovah Shalom - The Lord is Peace.

He is Jehovah Rapha – The Lord Heals. He is Jehovah Rohi – The Lord is My Shepherd. He is!!!!!! Do you believe He is? If so, who is He to you?

C. He is a rewarder of them that diligently seek Him.

Merriam Webster's definition of diligent is to be characterized by steady, earnest and energetic effort. Her pace was steady; her desire for healing was earnest and she used what energy that she had left to make her way to him.

She didn't casually seek Him. She was diligent. She was intentional. She knew that she needed help and she purposefully sought Him out. She knew He would have what she needed.

She had looked for help in other places and other people and had come up short. If she had sought Him sooner could her suffering have ended sooner. Was it necessary for her to hurt and be in pain for 12 long years? Could she have received healing before now? Have you suffered longer than necessary? How many other remedies have you tried before going to God? Have you tried to solve your issues yourself, in your own might and in your own strength and came up short?

Not by might nor by power, but by my Spirit,' *says the Lord Almighty*. Zechariah 4:6

At some point we must let our faith kick in and seek Him and quit seeking after men. Men that don't always have our best interest at heart. Truth be told, we've wasted too much time chasing after people that would end up hurting, using or abusing us. It's time out for making people a priority when you are only an option in their life. You've put others first, but at some point, you must take care of you.

You must get the help you need to get better. She diligently sought after Him and found out that He is a rewarder of them that diligently seek Him. She was rewarded with her healing. Who have you been seeking for help with your issues? Have you sought Him? Have you sought Him diligently? Have you been rewarded? What was the reward?

If God has given us His word (made us a promise) that He would reward us, why would we not diligently (steady, earnest and with energetic effort) seek Him? What has God promised you? Have you received it? If not, is it because you have failed to seek Him diligently? Make up in your mind that you're going to "*trust in the LORD with all thine heart; and LEAN NOT unto THINE OWN UNDERSTANDING. In all thy ways acknowledge him, and he shall direct thy paths."* (Proverbs 3:5-6)

Lord, help me to please you first and foremost. Help me to seek you, your kingdom and your righteousness and then all other things will be added (given) to me. What things will be added? ALL I need. Friendships. Relationships. Marriage. Finances. Health. Peace. If I seek God and seek to please Him, he will reward me with the things and people that He knows I need.

Faith is the substance of things hoped for, the evidence of things not seen (Hebrews 11:1). This woman with the issue of blood had hoped to be healed for twelve years and although she hadn't seen the healing, she believed that she would be. She had hope. She had faith to believe if Jesus had healed others, He could do the same for her.

For we walk by faith, not by sight. 2 Corinthians 5:7

If she had waited to see the healing, she might still be bleeding/hurting but she moved in faith. Like her, we must have faith and trust that God can heal whatever ails or is hurting us, whether it be mentally, physically or spiritually. We must have faith to believe He can fix whatever is broke. We must have faith if we want to please God.

My faith and prayer life started small but it grew

over the years. With every heartbreak I prayed and my faith grew. With every trial I prayed and my faith grew. With every setback I prayed and my faith grew. I've been praying for as long as I've been living. I remember earnestly praying around the age of 8 and having a strong belief that God was listening.

From that day forward, I've always prayed, believing that God was listening and waiting to respond. I often ask people, "why pray if you don't believe God is going to answer?" Your belief should match your behavior. If you pray in faith, then walk and act as if God has heard and will respond. My faith has grown tremendously through the years. I believe in the power of prayer because I know what prayer can do. I've prayed and seen the sick healed; finances increased; my children saved; loved ones delivered; my enemies stopped in their tracks and captives set free.

I've prayed and received clarity, direction, elevation, revelation, restoration, forgiveness and healing. He's faithful to His word. There was a verse in an old gospel song that said, "You can't make me doubt him, I know too much about him." Even if I don't see an immediate change in my situation I know he is behind the scenes working on my behalf.

It's been said, "no prayer – no power; little prayer – little power; much prayer – much power!"

I know that the power is not in me or the prayer itself but in the one to whom I'm praying. Even when the answer I receive is not the one I am expecting, I have faith to believe it is the one that God knows is best for me.

On a scale of 1 to 10, 10 being the worst, how would you rate your level of pain? _____

On a scale of 1 to 10, 10 being the worst, how would I rate my level of pain?   1

> *I'm no longer bleeding, hiding*
> *or keeping secrets.*
> *I have an identity. I'm healed.*

CHAPTER 11: NO MORE PAIN AND SUFFERING

"……. Go in peace and **be freed from your suffering.**" Verse 34b

As I closed chapter 10, I stated that I'm no longer bleeding, hiding or keeping secrets. I have an identity and my body has been healed. If all this has taken place, then why am I acknowledging that my level of pain is still rated one and not completely gone? What's left? Was the healing not complete? Will I never be totally healed? What's wrong with me? Am I still broken? Jesus doesn't leave me wondering and asking questions for long. He tells me the very words that He told her…… *"Go in peace and be freed from your suffering."*

Go in peace. Rest your mind. No longer did she have to experience doubt, discomfort, depression, anxiety, unhappiness, misery, pain or suffering because of this issue. No longer did she have to be the victim. No longer would her past dictate her future.

She had been freed from her suffering. Jesus understood what she had endured. He knew she had been in bondage for way too long. Go in peace. Peace. She had sought Him, and He rewarded her with healing and peace. He promised to give peace and He had kept His promise. Peace. Not just any peace *but the peace of God, which surpasses all understanding.* (Philippians 4:7a). Peace! We all want and need it. We don't realize how much we need it until life is filled with chaos.

Life had truly been chaotic for her. It had been full of confusion for so long and now she was being given peace. She didn't have to spend a dime. It was given to her. It was hers – free of charge (or at least no cost to her). It was a gift from Him to her. No strings attached. No bargaining. No bartering. No quid pro quid (do that for me and I'll do this for you). He had given her the gift of peace.

The struggle had been real. She considered everything that she had been through up to that point. She recalled all of the abuse, the disappointments, the lies that were told to her and the ones told on her; the rejection she had experienced from family and friends; the depression she had suffered; the mental anguish; the sleepless nights, the tear stained pillows; the loneliness; the addictions; the cheating; the promiscuity; the compromises she had made; the masks she had worn trying to cover up her emotional mess; the hurtful words spoken to or about her; the thoughts and even attempts at suicide.

It all came flooding to the forefront of her mind. She remembered it all, but at the sound of His voice and the words that were spoken, she let it all go. She laid all the hurt, the pain, the suffering at His feet. He said, "Go," but she initially heard "Come!" *"Come to me, all who are weary and heavy-laden and I will give you rest."* She exchanged her garment of heaviness that had worn her down for so long for His garment of peace. He let her know that her pain and suffering and all her tears had not been in vain. *"They that sow in tears shall reap in joy."*

Psalm 126:5

Life hadn't always treated her kind, but she had continued to move. She hadn't allowed herself to stay stuck. At times it felt as though she wasn't living but merely existing. She knew there was more to life than her past predicament. She just hadn't known how to get what she needed. Everything she had tried before Him had failed. He gave her an invitation to go in peace. Sometimes we get up enough strength and determination to go, but we don't go with peace and while we may not physically be with the individual we have allowed them to keep us in bondage. Stuck. Still thinking about old memories, still watching good times instead of having good times.

Don't go with the weight and heaviness of your past; lay that down. Go! Don't go with jealousy that she has what you could've had by now. What God has for you it is for you. Go! Don't go with frustration that you've missed out on anything. Delayed doesn't mean denied. Go! God will restore what the enemy stole. Go! Don't go with doubt.

He's healed you and prepared you for such a time as this. Don't go with unforgiveness or a hardened heart. Go in peace. Don't just go; go with his blessing of peace. John 14:27 *Peace I leave with you; my peace I give you. I do not give you as the world gives. Do not let your hearts be troubled and do not be afraid."*

He had healed her body and was now healing her mind and soul. *"So, if the Son sets you free, you will be free indeed."* (John 8:36). Jesus would not do as some of her doctors had previously done and only partially healed her. He would do a complete work - inside and out. Some of us will go to the doctor to see about what ails us in the body but we neglect the mind and soul. We're ashamed to talk to a doctor about emotional illnesses for fear someone will think something is wrong with us, when in fact it is. We're prideful, embarrassed or ashamed so we walk around broken and not whole. What you probably don't realize is that the people that you're probably trying to impress have either sought help, on meds or have a ton of issues themselves that they're hiding from you or not dealing with. Remember, we're being delivered from what people say and think about us. We're getting everything we need in this season.

As we prepare to close this part of our journey, what have we learned? What have we discovered about ourselves? What changes have we made or still need to make? What setbacks were there? What victories have been experienced? As you complete this book but continue on your journey of healing, I want to leave you with a few tips or suggestions that helped me during my process.

Journal your journey. Keep a daily journal. You determine when you write. In the mornings, you might write your thoughts and plans for the day. At night, I've found it helpful to recap the events of the day by listing accomplishments as well as setbacks and other thoughts.

Pray about the issues/struggles that you've identified.

Be determined to make the necessary changes (cut ties, delete/block phone numbers, confide in someone, seek professional help, etc.).

Find an accountability partner who you trust that will help you stay true to your plans and goals. You're not looking for a yes man/woman but someone who will be honest with you that will push and encourage you to be your best.

Confide in someone that is mature and wise to share your journey of healing with (this may be someone other than your accountability partner).

Celebrate your accomplishments (no matter how small) with family and friends that will rejoice with you.

Take time for yourself doing things you like and don't feel guilty about doing so.

Remain positive. If you fall, get up! Try again.

Don't sweat the small stuff.

Laugh – even if it's at yourself.

Exercise your mind, body and soul.

Memorize scriptures to keep your mind focused.

Take time to be still and be quiet (doing absolutely nothing). You might be surprised how much you gain in silence.

Surround yourself with people who don't just tolerate you but appreciate and celebrate you.

Do something different. If you always go that route, try another one. The change of scenery might open your eyes to something new.

Be flexible – don't be so predictable and set in your ways.

Try something new- you might gain a new hobby or skill.

Don't stop learning (read a book, take a class, etc.).

Volunteer (it helps you and others).

Stay motivated (even if you have to encourage yourself).

Keep moving forward. You're closer to your destiny than you were yesterday.

Jesus completely healed her and wants to do the same for me and for you. He doesn't want us hurting. He doesn't want us in bondage to anyone or anything. When God gave me the title for this book, The Broken Rib, I was single. That was over 15 years ago and I'm still unmarried. It wasn't until I began writing that I realized that I was this woman with the issue of blood and that the depth of my hurt wasn't new but something that I had been dealing with for a very long time. Don't misunderstand me; I haven't been single the entire time. I've dated during those years. Some good – some not so good. I've learned a lot through these dating experiences. I've learned that hurting people hurt people, whether intentional or otherwise.

I've learned that no matter how bad you want something or someone, you can't force it. I've learned you can't buy love. I've learned if God says no, you must trust Him, no matter how much it hurts. It will save you time, emotions and energy among other things.

As I've written this book, I've cried, grown and been healed. It's not always easy to look in a mirror and be shown all your flaws and imperfections. Not easy but necessary. I needed to know I was broken. How else could I get the healing that I needed? I needed to know that while I thought I was doing a good job of hiding my hurt that sometimes my actions allowed others to know that there was something slightly wrong and even if they didn't notice, God did. I needed to be reminded that I wasn't perfect. No one is. Like everyone else, I had and still have things that need to be worked on, fixed or changed. While I desire to be married, I have a greater desire to be in right relationship with God. When I spend time with Him, He shows me what I'm lacking.

The woman with the issue had been bleeding and hurting for 12 years. I've been trying to write this book even longer. Not realizing that God has literally been trying to heal me for at least that long. I cry today, not because I'm not healed but because of the process that I've been through. In an earlier chapter I wondered if this woman could have been healed sooner had she gone to the right place. Could I have? Could you have? Was I in denial that I needed help? Have you been? Did I seek help in all the wrong places? Have you? Did I compromise morals at the cost or expense of pleasing others?

Have you?

It wasn't until I read her story that I heard a voice inside of me saying, "He wants to help you too! He wants to stop the bleeding. He doesn't want you to continue this cycle. He doesn't want you to devalue yourself just for the sake of being in a relationship. He needs you to know His voice. He has more for you. He desires more for you and wants you to desire more for yourself. You don't have to remain broken. You don't have to continue to hide. He needs you to press pass the pain. He wants to heal you. He's preparing you for something and someone greater." *"Eye has not seen, nor ear heard, nor have entered into the heart of man the things which God has prepared for those who love Him."* 1Corinithians 2:9 NKJV

I no longer have to settle. I no longer choose to compromise. I no longer have to hide my pain or remain silent. I have a voice. I will use it to speak life into my situation. I no longer have low self-esteem, fear or doubt. I will no longer force myself to remain in places I don't belong (not in a relationship, on a job, on a committee, etc.). I will no longer be the broken rib. He has healed me. I have decided to go in peace and be freed from my suffering. Those were my words. That was my declaration.

Now, with a mirror in hand or in front of you, look in it and boldly tell yourself, "I no longer have to settle. I no longer choose to compromise. I no longer have to hide my pain or remain silent. I have a voice. I will use it to speak life into my situation. I no longer have low self-esteem, fear or doubt. I will no longer force myself to remain in places I don't belong (not in a relationship, on a job, on a committee, etc.). I will no longer be the broken rib. He has healed me. I have decided to go in peace and be freed from my suffering."

On a scale of 1 to 10, 10 being the worst, how would you rate your level of pain? _____

On a scale of 1 to 10, 10 being the worst, how would I rate my level of pain?

Today, I have no pain! My relationships with God, myself, my dad and others have all been restored. I'm no longer bleeding, hiding or keeping secrets. I have an identity. My mind, body and soul have been healed. I'm just here for a follow-up visit to show you I'm no longer The Broken Rib.

I've moved from hemorrhaging to healing!

CHAPTER 12: THERE'S HEALING IN HIS WORD

Go in peace and be freed from your suffering.

Verse 34b

Go in peace. There is true healing that can be found in the Word of God. It was the word of God that sustained, delivered and healed me. God's word is a refuge and fortress. His word has protected me, comforted and guided me. *"He that dwelleth in the secret place of the Most High shall abide under the shadow of the Almighty. I will say of the Lord, He is my refuge and my fortress; my God; in Him will I trust."* Psalm 91:1 KJV

It is not enough for us to read scripture we should meditate on it day and night. All the answers that we're searching for can be found in His word.

Study this Book of Instruction continually. Meditate on it day and night so you will be sure to obey everything written in it. Only then will you prosper and succeed in all you do. Joshua 1:8 NLT

Throughout the chapters of this book, there were scriptures listed that have ministered to me as I journeyed from hemorrhaging to healing. I have listed those verses and pray that as you continue your journey to healing and attaining all that God has for you that they will also be motivation and encouragement for you.

You will notice that some chapters had multiple scriptures, some had a couple and some had only one. I was going to go back and add an additional verse or two, but God convicted me. He said to leave it as is and to emphasize that's what I've done on this journey, but that I'm not alone. There are those chapters in our lives that we either don't do it at all or barely read, trust, have faith in or stand on His word. We rely on ourselves or the thoughts, advice and opinions of others. It is my prayer that we will consistently seek God, study His word and apply it to our lives so that we can walk in the peace and joy that He desires for us. As we stand on His word and His promises, we will see that God is able to restore everything that the enemy has stolen from us and even the things that we gave away.

For I will restore health unto thee, and I will heal thee of thy wounds, saith the Lord. Jeremiah 30:17 KJV

AFTERWORD

Thank you for taking this journey from hemorrhaging to healing with me. This book was written to minister to:

The single woman who's been hurt by Mr. Wrong yet she's still waiting for Mr. Right

The woman whose injuries were self-inflicted because she didn't know her worth

The divorcee' who may be struggling with her identity now that she is no longer attached

The widow who may have lost hope and feels displaced

The guy who is a good man and has yet to find his mate because she's one of the above

The man who recognizes, realizes and repents for contributing to a broken rib

The wife whose husband has forgotten the sacred vows he took to love and protect her when he claimed her as his rib

The woman that injured a man not realizing she was forcing herself where she didn't fit or belong

To anyone that has suffered silently; wrestled with feeling broken or thought that you or your story were insignificant or irrelevant

The Broken Rib, discussed the problems of the woman with the issue of blood while addressing my own personal struggles with being a single woman. It is my hope that after reading her story and my story, you were able to examine your own. I pray that you have addressed and not overlooked your issues; evaluated relationships and gained strength to walk away from the ones that have harmed or hurt you; found someone you can trust to talk to about those deep or dark issues that haunt you; found your voice and will use it to speak life over yourself and others; discovered your true identity; increased your faith and will share it with others; and if you didn't have a relationship with God before now that you will talk to someone about having one. If he restored her and healed me, know that he wants to do the same for you. Whether you or male or female, young or old, single or married, black or white, Christian or non-Christian, no longer will you be broken.

My purpose for writing this book was two-fold: Obedience and Transparency. God's purpose for me writing was also two-fold: Deliverance and Healing. God needed me to trust and obey. I couldn't be concerned with what you would think or say. I just had to be real – open and honest in hopes that someone might receive their healing. Because I obeyed, not only did I receive deliverance and healing, but as I was seeking God, Mr. Right was also seeking and has found me! Found me healthy and whole. No longer bleeding. No longer the broken rib. God's timing is perfect! I encourage you to wait on God as you move from hemorrhaging to healing!

But they that wait upon the LORD shall renew their strength; they shall mount up with wings as eagles; they shall run, and not be weary; and they shall walk, and not faint. Isaiah 40:31 KJV

WHILE SEARCHING FOR YOU

While searching for you I saw the little girl that was waiting for her dad to return

While searching for you my heart constantly ached and my soul would often yearn

While searching for you I ran into that teen girl that had sought for attention

While searching for you I slept with others whose name I won't dare mention

While searching for you I heard ridiculous lie after lie and fib after fib

While searching for you I became damaged and ultimately the broken rib

While searching for you I continued to try to fit where I didn't belong

While searching for you I finally found the songbird who had lost her song

While searching for you I let go of old baggage, heartache and pain

While searching for you it was then that I learned how to dance in the rain

While searching for you layers of unforgiveness, guilt and shame began to peel

While searching for you I realized it was God's touch I desperately longed to feel

While searching for you there was so much about myself God needed to reveal

While searching for you I was finally set free, delivered and able to heal

While searching for you I stood and stared in a mirror and clearly began to see

That all the while I had been searching for you I had finally found the real me

SCRIPTURE REFERENCE

INTRODUCTION

"Then the Lord God said, "It is not good that the man should be alone; I will make him a helper fit for him. So, the Lord God caused a deep sleep to fall upon the man, and while he slept took one of his ribs and closed up its place with flesh. And the rib that the Lord God had taken from the man he made into a woman and brought her to the man." Genesis 2:18, 21-22

He who finds a wife finds a good thing and finds favor with the Lord. Proverbs 18:22

The steps of a [good and righteous] man are directed and established by the LORD, And He delights in his way [and blesses his path]. Psalm 37:23

Heal me, O Lord, and I shall be healed; save me, and I shall be saved: for thou art my praise. Jeremiah 17:14

CHAPTER 1   **What's Your Issue?**

For I know the plans I have for you declares the Lord, plans to prosper you and not to harm you, plans to give you hope and a future. Jeremiah 29:11

I shall not die, but live, and declare the works of the Lord. Psalm 118:17

Weeping may endure for a night but joy cometh in the morning. Psalm 30:5

CHAPTER 2   **Getting Worse**
                       Instead of Better

We are hard pressed on every side, but not crushed, perplexed, but not in despair, persecuted but not abandoned, struck down but not destroyed. 2Corinthians 4:8

CHAPTER 3   **Press Your Way**
                       Through

He is not man that he should lie. Numbers 23:19

CHAPTER 4   **Keep Hope Alive**

For as a man thinketh, so is he. Proverbs 23:7

I can do all things through Christ who strengthens me. Philippians 4:13

Now faith is the substance of things hoped for and the evidence of things not seen. Hebrews 11:1

If then you were raised with Christ, seek those things which are above, where Christ is, sitting at the right hand of God. 2 Set your mind on things above, not on things on the earth. Colossians 3:1-2

Therefore, prepare your minds for action; be self-controlled; set your hope fully on the grace to be given when Jesus Christ is revealed. 1Peter 1:13

Finally, brothers and sisters, whatever is true, whatever is noble, whatever is right, whatever is pure, whatever is lovely, whatever is admirable—if anything is excellent or praiseworthy—think about such things. Philippians 4:8

I shall not die but live, and will proclaim what the Lord has done! Psalm 118:17

Death and life are in the power of the tongue: and they that love it shall eat the fruit thereof. Proverbs 18:21

Do you want to get well? John 5:6

CHAPTER 5   **The Bleeding**
Has Stopped

Faith without works is dead. James 2:26

The thief comes only to steal, and to kill, and to destroy. I am come that they may have life, and that they may have it abundantly. John 10:10

I will give you the keys (authority) of the kingdom of heaven; and whatever we bind [forbid, declare to be improper and unlawful] on earth will have [already] been bound in heaven, and whatever you loose [permit, declare lawful] on earth will have [already] been loosed in Heaven. Matthew 16:19

You intended to harm me, but God intended it for good to accomplish what is now being done, the saving of many lives. Genesis 50:20

No weapon formed against you will prosper; And every tongue that accuses you in judgment you will condemn. This is the heritage of the servants of the Lord, and their vindication is from Me. declares the Lord. Isaiah 54:17

For I am confident of this very thing, that He who began a good work in you will perfect it until the day of Christ Jesus. Philippians 1:6

CHAPTER 6   A Secret Touch

Seek ye first the kingdom of God and his righteousness and then all these things shall be added unto you. Matthew 6:33

CHAPTER 7   You Can't Hide Forever

"...Greater is He that's within me than He's that's in this world." 1John 4:4

CHAPTER 8   No More Secrets

The LORD is close to the brokenhearted and saves those who are crushed in spirit. Psalm 34:8

If we confess our sins, he is faithful and just to forgive our sins, and to cleanse us from all unrighteousness. 1John 1:9

Seek ye first the kingdom of God and his righteousness and then all these things shall be added unto you. Matthew 6:33

Casting all your cares [all your anxieties, all your worries, and all your concerns, once and for all] on Him, for /he cares about you [with deepest affection, and watches over you very carefully]. 1Peter 5:7

But he said to me, "My grace is sufficient for you, for my power is made perfect in weakness." Therefore, I will boast all the more gladly about my weaknesses, so that Christ's power may rest on me. 2 Corinthians 12:9

Thou wilt keep him in perfect peace, whose mind is stayed on thee: because he trusteth in thee. Isaiah 26:3

 He that dwelleth in the secret place of the most High shall abide under the shadow of the Almighty. 2 I will say of the LORD, He is my refuge and my fortress: my God; in him will I trust. Psalm 91:1-2

For God has not given us a spirit of fear, but of power and of love and of a sound mind. 2Timothy 1:7

A time to keep silence, and a time to speak.

Ecclesiastes 3:7b

And Jesus looking upon them saith, "With men it is impossible, but not with God: for with God all things are possible." Mark 10:27

CHAPTER 9   True Identity Revealed

"And we know that all things work together for good..." Romans 8:28

My people are destroyed from lack of knowledge. Hosea 4:6

The Lord says, "forget what happened before, and do not think about the past. Look at the new thing I am going to do. It is already happening. Don't you see it? Isaiah 43:18-19a

CHAPTER 10   Faith Has Healed You

But without faith it is impossible to please him: for he that cometh to God must believe that He is, and that he is a rewarder of them that diligently seek Him. Hebrews 11:6

.... An ever-present help in trouble. Psalm 46:1

…Not by might nor by power, but by my Spirit, says the Lord Almighty. Zechariah 4:6

Trust in the LORD with all thine heart; and lean not unto thine own understanding. In all thy ways acknowledge him, and he shall direct thy paths. Proverbs 3:5-6

Now faith is the substance of things hoped for, the evidence of things not seen. Hebrews 11:1

God is not a man that He should lie. Numbers 23:19

For we walk by faith, not by sight. 2 Corinthians 5:7

CHAPTER 11   No More Pain
and Suffering

Peace of God, which surpasses all understanding. Philippians 4:7a

Come to me, all who are weary and heavy-laden and I will give you rest. Matthew11:28

They that sow in tears shall reap in joy." Psalm 126:5

Peace I leave with you; my peace I give you. I

do not give you as the world gives. Do not let your hearts be troubled and do not be afraid. John 14:27

So, if the Son sets you free, you will be free indeed. John 8:36

Eye has not seen, nor ear heard, nor have entered into the heart of man the things which God has prepared for those who love Him. 1Corinithians 2:9

CHAPTER 12   There's Healing in His Words

He that dwelleth in the secret place of the Most High shall abide under the shadow of the Almighty. I will say of the Lord, He is my refuge and my fortress; my God; in Him will I trust. Psalm 91:1

Study this Book of Instruction continually. Meditate on it day and night so you will be sure to obey everything written in it. Only then will you prosper and succeed in all you do. Joshua 1:8

For I will restore health unto thee, and I will heal thee of thy wounds, saith the Lord. Jeremiah 30:17

But they that wait upon the LORD shall renew their strength; they shall mount up with wings as eagles; they shall run, and not be weary; and they shall walk, and not faint. Isaiah 40:31

ABOUT THE AUTHOR

Minister Rhonda M. Joseph serves as an assistant minister at St. Stephen Church, Louisville, Kentucky, under the leadership of Rev. Dr. Kevin W. Cosby, Senior Pastor, where she has been a member since January, 2010. She is the Director of the Prayer Ministry. She is the primary intercessor for the assistant minster team and is the captain for a team of minsters that serves at Dosker Manor, an assisted living facility. She is also a regular participant of One Voice One Prayer Movement and a student at Simmons College of Kentucky taking Religious Studies.

Minister Rhonda is an evangelist, who began preaching and teaching the Word of God in September, 2005. She has facilitated Women's Ministry workshops and conferences all for the glory of God. She is an active participant of Sister to Sister, which is a women's fellowship that meets monthly and is aimed at encouraging, embracing and empowering women to walk in their purpose.

Rhonda is an enthusiastic member of the Jail/Prison Ministry, where she has served regularly for the last thirteen years.

Rhonda's passion is to minister to women as well as to those who are incarcerated. She ministers at both men and women's correctional facilities. She wants them to know that they may be locked up, but are not locked out from God's love. Others may see them as incarcerated and outcasts, but she reminds them that they are included in and not cast out from God's plans and promises.

Minister Rhonda loves the Lord and is humbled each time He chooses to use her to minister or serve in any capacity. She has experienced the power of the shed blood of Jesus Christ in her life, time and time again.

Her experiences have developed within her certain sensitivities to those suffering, and she desires to do all necessary in accordance with Luke 4:18-19, which states: *The Spirit of the Lord is upon me, because he hath anointed me to preach the gospel to the poor; he hath sent me to heal the brokenhearted, to preach deliverance to the captives, and recovering of sight to the blind, to set at liberty them that are bruised, To preach the acceptable year of the Lord.*

Her message to the downtrodden everywhere is simple: Jesus cares, He saves and He loves you.

She is the mother of three sons, Cameron, Brandon and James and the proud grandmother of her one and only granddaughter, Jordyn Janay.

If you forget her name or title, just tell them: She was just somebody, trying to tell everybody about somebody who could save anybody.

.

Made in the USA
Monee, IL
17 August 2020